Yokohama Street Life

Asia World
Series Editor: Mark Selden

This series charts the frontiers of Asia in global perspective. Central to its concerns are Asian interactions—political, economic, social, cultural, and historical—that are transnational and global, that cross and redefine borders and networks, including those of nation, region, ethnicity, gender, technology, and demography. It looks to multiple methodologies to chart the dynamics of a region that has been the home to major civilizations and is central to global processes of war, peace, and development in the new millennium.

Titles in the Series

Water: The Looming Crisis in India, by Binayak Ray
Windows on the Chinese World: Reflections by Five Historians, by Clara Wingchung Ho
Tommy's Sunset, by Hisako Tsurushima
Lake of Heaven: An Original Translation of the Japanese Novel by Ishimure Michiko, by Bruce Allen
Imperial Subjects as Global Citizens: Nationalism, Internationalism, and Education in Japan, by Mark Lincicome
Japan in the World: Shidehara Kijūrō, Pacifism, and the Abolition of War, Volumes I and II, by Klaus Schlichtmann
Filling the Hole in the Nuclear Future: Art and Popular Culture Respond to the Bomb, edited by Robert Jacobs
Radicalism, Revolution and Reform in Modern China: Essays in Honor of Maurice Meisner, edited by Catherine Lynch, Robert B. Marks, and Paul G. Pickowicz
The "Other" Karen in Myanmar: Ethnic Minorities and the Struggle without Arms, by Ardeth Thawnghmung
A Localized Culture of Welfare: Entitlements, Stratification, and Identity in a Chinese Lineage Village, by Kwok-shing Chan
Malay Kingship in Kedah: Religion, Trade, and Society, by Maziar Mozaffari Falarti
Refining Nature in Modern Japanese Literature: The Life and Art of Shiga Naoya, by Nanyan Guo
Heritage Politics: Shuri Castle and Okinawa's Incorporation into Modern Ja-pan, 1879–2000, by Tze May Loo
Yokohama Street Life: The Precarious Career of a Japanese Day Laborer, by Tom Gill

Yokohama Street Life

The Precarious Career of a Japanese Day Laborer

Tom Gill

LEXINGTON BOOKS
Lanham • Boulder • New York • London

Published by Lexington Books
An imprint of The Rowman & Littlefield Publishing Group, Inc.
4501 Forbes Boulevard, Suite 200, Lanham, Maryland 20706
www.rowman.com

Unit A, Whitacre Mews, 26-34 Stannary Street, London SE11 4AB

This book was published with the assistance of a grant from the Meiji Gakuin University fund for the promotion of scholarly research, financial year 2014.

British Library Cataloguing in Publication Information Available

Library of Congress Cataloging-in-Publication Data

Gill, Tom, 1960-
Yokohama street life : the precarious career of a Japanese day laborer / Tom Gill.
p. cm. — (Asiaworld)
Includes bibliographical references and index.
ISBN 978-1-4985-1198-8 (cloth : alk. paper) — ISBN 978-1-4985-1199-5 (electronic) 1. Day laborers—Japan—Yokohama-shi—Social conditions. 2. Working poor—Japan—Yokohama-shi—Social conditions. 3. Yokohama-shi (Japan)—Social conditions—21st century. 4. Yokohama-shi (Japan)—Economic condtions—21st century. I. Title.
HD5854.2.J3G554 2015
311.5'44—dc23
2014047130

™ The paper used in this publication meets the minimum requirements of American National Standard for Information Sciences Permanence of Paper for Printed Library Materials, ANSI/NISO Z39.48-1992.

Printed in the United States of America

Contents

Acknowledgments

This book has been a long time in the making and I would like to thank the many people who helped to make it happen. Norikazu Todoroki helped me interview Kimitsu on one occasion and also helped me with the text of the Japanese edition. Jun'ichi Machida and Yoshinari Morita also helped me prepare the Japanese edition on which the present English edition is based. Kyōhei Ogawa of Kyōtotto Press put a huge amount of work into improving the manuscript.

In preparing the English edition, I have been greatly indebted to Edward B. Fowler, professor emeritus of the University of California at Irvine, who carefully read through two versions of the manuscript and made many valuable suggestions to improve it. During a period as a visiting researcher at the Nissan Institute of Japanese Studies at Oxford University, I also received very useful feedback from Oxford University professor emeritus Arthur Stockwin and from Oxford University professor Ian Neary.

Later on in the process, Professor Mark Selden, Senior Research Associate in the East Asia Program at Cornell University and Emeritus Professor of History and Sociology at Binghamton University, read the manuscript, suggested many improvements, and finally recommended the book to Lexington for publication in his AsiaWorld series. Lexington editor Brian Hill and his assistant Brighid Klick have been very kind and helpful in guiding the book through to publication and I am most grateful to them and to all the staff at Lexington Books.

The cover photograph was taken in 1994 by Hideji Umetani. I thank him for granting permission to use it on this book as well as on the Japanese edition.

Publication of this book was expedited by a publication grant from my employers, Meiji Gakuin University, for which I am deeply grateful.

I have been supported throughout by my wife Manami, who has got to know Kimitsu very well and has been a good friend to him as well as being an essential partner to me.

Finally, I have to thank one person more than any other—Norimitsu "Kimitsu" Nishikawa himself, for sharing his time and his conversation with me, and for graciously giving me permission to publish his drawings and photos of him in the present work.

Tom Gill

In this volume, Japanese names have been written in Western order—personal name followed by family name.

Introduction

I am an Englishman who has lived in Japan for some twenty-five years. In my experience, Japanese people are rarely inclined to talk to strangers. But my friend Kimitsu Nishikawa is different. Walking along the street, he will offer hearty greetings to total strangers. He inclines his head forward, waves his hand near his head in a shaky karate chop salutation, and says "oh!"—which is the simplest greeting in the Japanese language. He loves children, and if one comes near, he will promptly pat it on the head. (A frightened mother pulls the child away.) When talking to me he sometimes struggles to recall a name or historical detail, and if I am not sure either, he will turn to a young lady waiting for the traffic lights to change and say "Excuse me, but can you remind me who became prime minister of England after Harold MacMillan? Was it Harold Wilson? Or was it Edward Heath?" (The young lady pretends she hasn't heard him.) If Kimitsu sees a great big sumo wrestler type man coming down the street, he finds it so amusing that he bursts out laughing and points at the man. (The man is angry, of course, but he lets it pass. It is a wonder that Kimitsu does not get beaten up more often, and a tribute to the gentle tolerance of so many Japanese people. If he had been born in a rougher country, he would have been beaten to death long ago.)

Kimitsu is often ignored, and gets quite a few funny looks. He does not care. Or rather, he does not notice. He lives in his own world, and it is not quite like ours. Partly it is because he tends to be drunk most of the time. He will take a swig of *shōchū*, a rough, barley-based liquor, and call it "the taste of honey." And then he'll sing the pop song with that title. One time he had a swig of Jinro—a brand of Korean shōchū. He said it went down very smoothly—"like the George Shearing quintet playing 'September in the Rain.'" He loves smooth jazz, and hard bop too.

There is a famous character in Turkish folklore called Nasreddin, whose friends used to say that he was "either the world's wisest fool, or the world's most foolish wise man." In the twenty-one years I have known Kimitsu Nishikawa, I have sometimes had the same thought about him.

I first encountered Kimitsu while researching day-laboring districts—proletarian urban centers called *yoseba* (workers' gathering places) or *doya-gai* (flophouse towns). My main field site has been Kotobuki, the Yokohama doya-gai. I published a book on the subject in 2001, based on my doctoral dissertation and entitled *Men of Uncertainty: The Social Organization of Day Laborers in Contemporary Japan* (Albany: SUNY Press). Day laborers have a certain look about them—weathered faces, blue overalls, baseball caps, broken-down sneakers, sometimes a slightly crabbed way of walking from industrial accidents. From a distance, they blend together. But seen up-close, and listened to at length, they emerge as unique individuals, each with his own story to tell. Those differences tend to get played down in an academic dissertation, which inevitably looks for commonality and generalization in order to describe a social phenomenon. In my book I tried to compensate for this by including eight brief vignettes—character sketches of some of the men I met in Kotobuki. That was an uneasy compromise, but in the present

Figure 0.1. A Friendly Greeting.

volume, my aim is to do the job properly: giving the reader a really close-up view of just one particular day laborer whom I have known for twenty-one years, named Kimitsu Nishikawa. You can find him on pages 168–170 of *Men of Uncertainty*, but I have gotten to know him a lot better since then. So taking my cue from anthropological masterpieces like Marjorie Shostak's *Nisa: The Life and Words of a !Kung Woman* (Harvard University Press, 1981) and Vincent Crapanzano's *Tuhami: Portrait of a Moroccan* (Chicago University Press, 1985), each of which also focused on a single informant, my aim here is to draw the reader into the life of an individual who, while unique, also offers insights into the society that made him.

There are eight thousand very similar metal doors in the flophouses of Kotobuki. Let us knock on just one of them, and see who we meet.

Chapter One

Kimitsu Nishikawa and the Town of Kotobuki, 1993–1995

From May 1993 to March 1995, I spent nearly two years conducting fieldwork in Kotobuki, towards my doctoral dissertation on the topic of day laborers in urban Japan, later published as *Men of Uncertainty*. Kotobuki is one of three famous day-laboring districts in Japan, somewhat comparable to traditional American skid rows. The other two are San'ya in Tokyo and Kamagasaki in Osaka. They are called *doya-gai*, a *doya* being a cheap lodging house. It is a venerable piece of Japanese street slang—*yado*, meaning an inn, put back-to-front. These places are also called yoseba, literally a place for gathering people, meaning a place to gather workers. Around Japan there are street labor markets without lodging houses and lodging-house districts without labor markets, but San'ya, Kamagasaki, and Kotobuki are both yoseba and doya-gai. Let me briefly describe these three atmospheric towns, in all three of which Kimitsu has lived. More detailed descriptions may be found in *Men of Uncertainty*.

The place name "San'ya" means "mountain-valley," yet the town is located in a flat, featureless part of northeast central Tokyo, close to Minami-Senju station on the Hibiya subway line and JR Jōban/Narita line. It is a district with a very inauspicious past, having been the main execution site of Tokyo in the days of the Tokugawa shogunate when the city was still called Edo. To this day, one of the crossroads on the fringe of San'ya is called Namidabashi, meaning "Bridge of Tears," although there is no bridge or river there. This was the place where the families of the condemned would bid them a final farewell. San'ya overlaps with a district that was long associated with the outcast community once known as Eta or Hinin, and now known as Burakumin. It is also associated with prostitution, being adjacent to the

Yoshiwara red-light district, which is at the other end of the Iroha covered shopping arcade, where many of San'ya's homeless men sleep at night.

San'ya developed into a major day laboring district during the early twentieth century, and by the time of World War II was the third biggest behind Fukagawa-Honjō and Shibaura. It reemerged after being destroyed in the allied firebombing of Tokyo in 1945, and has been Tokyo's biggest day laboring district ever since. There are about 200 doya, some of them small family-run inns, others part of chains controlled by wealthy landlord families. Much of the labor market and much of the San'ya economy generally is under the influence of a powerful yakuza gang called the Kanamachi family, which has been affiliated with Japan's largest underworld syndicate, the Yamaguchi-gumi, since 2005.[1] Relations between yakuza and day-laboring activists have been haunted by two murders in the mid-1980s, when the Kanamachi killed independent filmmaker Mitsuo Satō (1984) and union activist Kyō'ichi Yamaoka (1986). These incidents occurred despite the fact that San'ya is heavily policed, with a "Mammoth police box" (*manmosu kōban*) located near its center. Day laborers will tell you that this is designed to control possible street riots by workers rather than illegal activities by yakuza. San'ya has a long history of rioting, although it has become rather quiet since the turn of the millennium due to the aging of its population and the steady shift from day labor to welfare—a general pattern in Japanese doya-gai.

Kamagasaki in Osaka is the biggest doya-gai in Japan, being about twice as big as San'ya and four times as big as Kotobuki, though even so it covers an area of only about 0.4 square kilometers. Its history as a day-laboring town dates from 1911, when the day-laboring population of a slum district called Nagamachi was relocated to Kamagasaki when Nagamachi was demolished to make way for an industrial exposition that would be attended by the emperor.

Approaching Kamagasaki from JR Shin-Imamiya station, one is immediately confronted by the Airin Public Labor Exchange, a huge, gray, cavernous building where jobs are negotiated face-to-face in a roofed courtyard area at street level while unemployment payments and other government support services are available upstairs. There are also little restaurants, newspaper stands, and so on. This was a very noisy place early in the morning in the 1990s, but most of the time it is eerily quiet. At times the Kamagasaki Day Laborer Union—Kamanichirō—has negotiated to allow homeless men to sleep in the ground floor area, and I have seen hundreds of men sleeping there on occasion.

Another landmark of Kamagasaki is Triangle Park, which has become a kind of homeless haven, complete with an outdoor public TV, set in a metal cabinet on a stout metal pillar. The local official who chooses the channel makes sure that the baseball is always showing when Osaka's beloved hometown team, the Hanshin Tigers, are playing.

There are numerous yakuza offices dotted around Kamagasaki, all of them affiliated directly or indirectly with the Yamaguchi-gumi. There are also numerous surveillance cameras, which are trained not on the yakuza offices but on areas where workers/residents gather, confirming the view from San'ya that the police are there to enforce social order rather than to combat organized crime.

Kotobuki, where Kimitsu has been living for the past twenty-five years, is the youngest and smallest of the three great yoseba/doya-gai. It was under U.S. military control until 1956 and had no Japanese population when the land was derequisitioned. A crowded, disorderly doya-gai had developed a couple of kilometers away at Sakuragi-chō, home to dockworkers servicing the Port of Yokohama, which was very busy processing emergency imports in the difficult years after the war. Cholera outbreaks, fires, and vociferous complaints from local shopkeepers were among the problems there. In the end the authorities simply transferred the doya-gai to Kotobuki, relocating the casual labor exchange in April 1959.

Just three hundred meters square, this zone of lumpen-proletariat culture is very clearly defined on the map: a couple of dozen blocks of lodging houses, bars and welfare facilities totally different in atmosphere from the surrounding townscape. Kotobuki is located in central Yokohama, close by famous tourist attractions such as the fashionable Motomachi shopping arcade, the baseball stadium, and Chinatown. One crucial fact about Kotobuki that differentiates it from the other two yoseba/doya-gai is that much of the property is owned by ethnic Koreans. They are so-called "Zainichi" Koreans. The word literally means "Japan-resident Koreans," but refers to very long-term residents—those who came over to Japan before and during World War II, and their descendants. Battling acute discrimination and grinding post-war poverty, the Korean community in Yokohama somehow managed to create its own niche in the city's economy, running most of the doya in Sakuragi-chō. When the city closed down that doya-gai, the owners were compensated by being enabled to build doya in Kotobuki. Korean landlords own the great majority of the doya to this day, although the town has attracted some Japanese capital in the last decade or so, as people have started to notice the profitability of running welfare facilities.

Partly because of its ethnic Korean connection, Kotobuki has tended to be more accepting of foreign workers than the other two yoseba/doya-gai. In the peak year of 2003 there were over 1,000 foreign workers living in Kotobuki. Two-thirds of them were Korean—the fact that the doya were mostly owned by fellow Koreans made it easier for them to enter Kotobuki. There were also distinct Filipino and Chinese communities. The numbers rapidly declined after that, however, and now there are fewer than one hundred foreigners living in Kotobuki.

Another feature of Kotobuki is its close association with the longshoring industry. This is what made Kimitsu love the place—the access it offered to dock work at the Port of Yokohama, which he found much more interesting and more financially rewarding than construction work, the main source of employment at the other two main yoseba.

There are a couple of famous songs celebrating the bluesy working man's lifestyle in the doya-gai. Kamagasaki has *Kamagasaki Ninjō* (The Humanity of Kamagasaki) by Eiji Mitsune (1967), while San'ya has *San'ya Blues*, by Nobuyasu Okabayashi (1968). No one has yet produced a popular song about Kotobuki, so at the karaoke bars Kimitsu and his workmates used to sing the other two songs and substitute the place names with "Kotobuki" in the lyrics.

Okabayashi's song was the inspiration for Edward Fowler to entitle his classic study of San'ya life *San'ya Blues: Laboring Life in Contemporary Tokyo* (Cornell University Press, 1998). Kotobuki has been the subject of three book-length studies: Carolyn S. Stevens' *On the Margins of Japanese Society: Volunteers and the Welfare of the Urban Underclass* (London: Routledge, 1997), which looks at some of the voluntary support groups operating in Kotobuki; Rey Ventura's *Underground in Japan* (London: Jonathan Cape, 1992), which is a vivid account of the lives of Filipino illegal immigrant workers in Kotobuki; and my own *Men of Uncertainty; The Social Organization of Day Laborers in Contemporary Japan*. To date, however, noone has published a book in English on the biggest doya-gai of them all, Kamagasaki.

The Yokohama casual labor market at Kotobuki was a lively early morning scene when I first got to know the place in 1993 through 1995. There were street corner recruiters out and about from before dawn. Their main competition, the casual labor exchange on the ground floor of the Labor Welfare Building, always opened at 6:15 a.m. and a couple of hours before then there would be hundreds of men milling around there trying to get jobs. When the shutters went up, that would be the cue for an almighty scrum as men battled to get their registration card through one of the holes in the window and into the hand of the official who would give him a contract. It was at this daily event that I first met Kimitsu on October 20, 1993, at about 6 o'clock in the morning. Let me quote from the field note I wrote that day:

> Back to the Center. Approaching shutter-up time. Met a man called NISHIKAWA KIMITSU. He asked my nationality and when I said "British," he leaned over and whispered gleefully in my ear: "Edward Heath!" Then he mimed playing the organ, conducting an orchestra, sailing a yacht—Heath's hobbies. Then he added: "Harold Wilson . . . James Callaghan . . . Harold

Macmillan." Laughter. Then he returned to Heath, speaking in broken English: "Heath . . . inflation going up and up . . . poor people much trouble . . . he say I have my private life!" (Mimes organ-playing, conducting and yacht again). "Hahaha!"

He showed me his day laborer unemployment insurance handbook; it had about 10 stamps in it for this month. He needed four or five more to maintain eligibility. "No good!" he exclaimed, lobbed it into the air and toe-punted it into touch as it came down. We were among a large crowd of men waiting for shutter-up: I counted at least 150.

When the shutters went up, there were no more than a dozen jobs lit up, and many men turned away at once, muttering about the awful state of the market.

I made to move on. Nishikawa leaned over one more time and whispered "Enoch Powell!"

After that, I met Kimitsu many more times around the casual labor exchange. He asked me what I was doing in Kotobuki, and I told him I was conducting fieldwork for a doctorate in social anthropology. He immediately asked whether I was a Malinowskian functionalist or a Lévi-Straussian structuralist. Luckily for me he was too busy rambling on himself to give me a chance to answer. He actually had a book of Lévi-Strauss's in his pocket, which embarrassingly enough I had never even heard of. It was *Le Regard Éloigné*, or "*Haruka Naru Shisen*" in Japanese.[2]

I learned about Kimitsu's philosophy of work. He said that getting a job at the casual labor exchange was a gamble—if you got lucky, you might get a ticket for a job. I objected: though it shared the uncertainty of gambling, the system seemed more like raw capitalism with the strong elbowing the weak aside in the daily battle to get employment. He admitted that it was a "survival game," but insisted that even so, there was solidarity among day laborers, since everyone knew the rules of that game. Certainly I did notice he and other day laborers engaged in friendly conversation while waiting for the shutters to go up, although they were in direct competition with each other. Kimitsu sardonically remarked that a bigger difference between day laboring and gambling was that rather than winning a sum of money, you won the right to do some very hard work.

Kimitsu's view of life in the doya-gai was inconsistent but always intriguing. One cold winter day in 1994 I took a professional magazine photographer into Kotobuki and he attempted to photograph the battle to get job contracts at the labor welfare center. There were a couple of dozen men waiting in front of the shutters, and one of them objected to being photographed: "Leave us in peace, it's got nothing to do with you!" [*Hottoite kure, omē to kankei nē darō*] he shouted. Another argued back: "He should take as many pictures as he likes. We want the truth of this tragic scene told to the world!" [*Don-don toreba ii'n dayo. Zehi kono sanjō no koto o sekai ni oshiete moraitai!*].

A different objection came from Kimitsu, who was in the crowd waiting for the shutters to go up. He didn't like the word *sanjō* [tragic scene]: "No," he called out, "this isn't a tragic scene. We're just ordinary guys" [*Iie, sanjō ja nai. Futsū na hito dake dayo*]. From his point of view, he and his mates waiting at the shutters were just trying to get a day's work. They had nothing to be ashamed of, and hence no need to object to being photographed.[3] At other times, however, he insisted that the doya-gai was like a prison camp—the only differences being the absence of walls and the fact that the inmates did not realize they were incarcerated:

> About ten minutes after the last job had gone, up rolled Nishikawa Kimitsu, stinking drunk and clutching a can of Asahi Ice Beer. "HAHAHAHAHAHA!" he laughed, bending his legs, clutching his sides and throwing back his head. "No jobs! No jobs! Look at the poor men! What are they going to do? It's a Nazi concentration camp here, but they don't know it! THEY DON'T KNOW IT!!" And he cackled uproariously again.[4]

That theme emerged the day we went to see the film *Schindler's List*. We were an hour late but the film still had plenty left to run. A quick swig of shōchū and in we went. A sick woman was just being shot in the head by an SS officer in the middle of the street. From then on the film was quite relentless. It reduced me to tears several times but Kimitsu was made of sterner stuff.

We walked back into Kotobuki and had a drink at a dive called Kuishimbō (the Glutton). Kimitsu said the scenes where the Nazis divided the Jews up into healthy ones to work in labor camps and unhealthy ones to send to their deaths reminded him of the attitude of employers and bureaucrats to workers in Kotobuki. The healthy ones were put to work and given enough in welfare benefits to maintain a basic level of fitness; the unhealthy ones got no work and almost no benefits, effectively being left to die. Indeed, that was how the day-laborer unemployment insurance system worked: if you could average at least thirteen days work a month, it would pay you 7,500 yen[5] a day when you did not work, but if you dropped below thirteen days a month, you lost your eligibility and were rapidly on your way to penury.

"But it's better in Kotobuki," he said, "because we can die by drinking alcohol. It's much nicer than a gas oven or a bullet through the brain." He raised his one-cup and laughed loudly.[6]

A one-cup, or *wankappu*, is a single sealed glass of saké or shōchū. The container is more like a jam jar than an elegant goblet. It typically costs a couple of hundred yen and the glass is tough enough to survive clunking out of a vending machine, which was where Kimitsu usually bought his.

Kimitsu used to average about 12,000 yen a day when he got work; somewhat more at the docks, sometimes less on construction sites. Today an unskilled day laborer might struggle to make 8 or 9,000 yen a day, for the economy has not been kind to the trade. On the docks he would unload consignments of bananas, soybeans, corn, and rice, often for a company called Dai-Ichi Senpaku (First Shipping). Often the grains came in 60-kilogram sacks—almost as much as Kimitsu weighed himself. He possessed a surprising strength for one of his slight build. He did well in 1994 out of the failure of the Japanese rice crop, which led to major imports of Thai rice. The coffee freighters paid the top longshoring rate: a fat 17,000 yen. He also unloaded paper pulp from Canada and newsprint from Hokkaido, along with frozen seafood and chicken on refrigerated ships from China. It was dangerous work: the floor was slippery with ice and heavy crates were stacked high and unstable. You got a parka to keep out the -30C temperature, but you had to ascend the steps out of the hold very slowly, otherwise the transition to normal temperatures would make your heart pound and could lead to a heart attack.

Dai-Ichi Senpaku also handled liquor shipments: Scotch whisky, French brandy, Budweiser Beer from the United States, Heineken from Holland, Guinness from Ireland, Carlsberg from Denmark, and so forth. I thought this would be Kimitsu's dream job, but he said the unloading operation was watched by hawk-like checkers, rendering pilferage virtually impossible.[7]

He referred to work on construction sites as *anahori* (digging holes), although he also mixed cement, broke up paving stones and hauled away the wreckage of demolished houses. He sometimes had to do rudimentary plumbing jobs too, which he disliked because they required skill. Though he generally disliked construction work, because it was badly paid and took him away from the sea, occasionally there was fun to be had:

> I had a job the other day scraping old tiles off the floor at a museum. It was great, I was left to do it just as I pleased, I could make patterns. A bit of creativity makes all the difference to work. I've known guys who make perfect circles when they dig holes, or dig in squares for a change sometimes. I've known guys who can stack coffee bags in beautiful mosaics.[8]

In the 1990s Kimitsu was struggling to get enough work, but it had not always been so. During the high-growth years the Port of Yokohama was exceedingly busy, and Kimitsu recalls working back-to-back shifts, day and night for two or three days at a stretch. Now those days were long gone, and he took whatever work he could get, from the labor exchanges or the *tehaishi* (street corner labor recruiters, often in the pay of yakuza).

I asked Kimitsu about his daily budget, and he drew up some accounts on the fly-leaf of his Lévi-Strauss book. He estimated his average income on a day when he got work at 12,000 yen. The doya cost 1,500 yen, his shōchū habit about the same (seven or eight one-cups at just under 200 yen each), and food again about the same. He mostly ate rice, pickled vegetables, and beef sashimi, his favorite delicacy. He didn't frequent bars and restaurants; he ate and drank in the street or in his room, and he mostly bought from the reasonably priced stalls in Kotobuki's now-defunct covered market. With total outgoings of about 5,000 yen, he should have a surplus of about 7,000 yen from an average day with work. And yet, he said, he usually woke up the next day with just one or two blue thousand-yen notes left in his pocket. "I have never been able to understand this mystery," he ruefully remarked. He needed to work roughly every other day. So long as he could maintain eligibility for the day-laborer unemployment insurance, by working at least thirteen days a month,[9] he could do okay. As mentioned above, the program pays 7,500 yen a day for weekdays where the holder is not employed. Assuming thirteen days' work and eight days claiming the benefit, the monthly math looks like this:

13 x 12,000	=	156,000 yen
8 x 7,500	=	60,000 yen
Total:		216,000 yen

That is over $2,000 at most recent exchange rates and noticeably better than an entry-level salary in a small construction company.

But if he falls below 13 days a month, he loses the unemployment payments and things get a lot grimmer:

12 x 12,000 yen = 144,000 yen

His income falls by a third and he has to be much more careful with his money. This was what Kimitsu was talking about when he said the system sustained the fit and killed off the unfit.

Kimitsu's daily rent of 1,500 yen paid for a room in a doya called the Daimaru No.1. Like all doya-dwellers, he had a little card issued to him each month with a grid of squares representing the days in the month. Every time he paid a night's rent, the *chōba-san* or concierge would put a red seal on the relevant square. Good tenants might have a week or two of future squares filled in. Bad tenants would have empty squares stretching into the past, or even more than one rent card.

Kimitsu told me a little about life in the Daimaru. Nearly everyone there was old, he said, and some were virtually bedridden. They lay there on their dirty futons, day in, day out, soaking up shōchū and talking, in great rambling monologues, mostly to themselves. Kimitsu knew that he himself was quite prone to monologues, which he viewed as a first sign of impending senility. He feared—and he illustrated this fear with actions—that it wouldn't be too long before he too was on his back, rambling about the state of the world and slobbering down his neck.

Kimitsu had a complex relationship with the Korean concierge at the Daimaru doya. Often he would be a couple of days late with the rent, and in September 1993, he told me, he'd slipped a whole week behind. When one is behind with the rent, it is important to avoid the concierge. In the September crisis, he was so terrified of her that he actually took to leaving the doya at 4 in the morning, when he could be fairly confident that the concierge would still be asleep, and went past the reception office on hands and knees, just in case she had got up early and was sitting behind the little glass window, ready to berate Kimitsu. On one occasion I myself felt the force of her fury, when she castigated both of us for taking a couple of guys up to his room from a film crew who were making a documentary. She threatened to throw Kimitsu out of his room.

What really impressed me here was Kimitsu's all-embracing tolerance. He stoutly defended the concierge when I called her a witch, saying that she was Korean and bore the scars of Japanese imperialism, civil war, and a divided motherland. Her paranoia was absolutely understandable. That accident-prone film crew had also been shoved around and told to leave by an unpleasant yakuza gangster, but Kimitsu defended him too: "Only doing his job," he remarked. "There could well be problems for the yakuza if some of their activities are broadcast on television, and they naturally do what they can to prevent this happening." I had noticed before that Kimitsu did not join in the common practice of condemning employers, yakuza, labor recruiters, and so forth. His position was that he was grateful if they had a job for him. This quality of tolerance, I felt, was the key to understanding Kimitsu Nishikawa and perhaps Kotobuki as well. People who would not fit in in other parts of the big city can find a place for themselves in the doya-gai—the good, the bad, and the ugly.

> We talked a bit more about yakuza. Kimitsu said they didn't bother him, they were just men, like any other men—60% water. Did I know that human beings were 60% water? Even the Archbishop of Canterbury! "In your case, 60% saké," I said. Kimitsu laughed his head off. "How about the Archbishop of Canterbury?" he asked. "Probably 60% port wine," I said. He laughed his head off again. I explained that port was the traditional tipple of the British aristocracy, and gout the traditional port-related ailment. Kimitsu found the word "gout" incredibly funny and wanted to know all about it. He deliberately mixed it up with "doubt" and imagined Hamlet suffering from it. I quoted Lytton Strachey's description of George IV—"bewigged and gouty, ornate and enormous"—and he loved that too. "They just get older and bigger and they can't move and their bones ache!" shouted Kimitsu, tears of laughter streaming down his face.[10]

Kimitsu was not always tolerant, however. He strongly identified with the regular people of Kotobuki—people who were all in the same boat and would help each other out when in difficulty—and resented outsiders. One time I introduced him to a newcomer called Manabu. Kimitsu took an immediate dislike to him: "I've never seen you before," he said. "What are you doing here, with those posh shoes?" He pointed accusingly at Manabu's shoes. "That's not the kind of shoes people wear here, look!" He pointed at the shoes of the men still milling around the shutters. Some were in rubber boots, some had old sneakers, and a few were in open sandals. "Are you a gangster or something?" "No, I'm a working man, same as you," said Manabu, showing Kimitsu the slip of paper he had obtained for a driving job. "If he's got a driving license, he should get a steady job somewhere else," Kimitsu said to me, but loud enough for Manabu to hear. "What have I got? I haven't got posh shoes, I haven't got a driving license, I've got nothing. This is a place for people who've got nothing. I hate people who come here *window-shopping*." He used the English expression.

Manabu tactfully withdrew. On his way off, he humorously mimed giving Kimitsu a punch in the face, a gesture which I saw but Kimitsu did not.[11]

In those days there were a lot of foreign workers operating out of Kotobuki, many of them illegal. As I mentioned, the biggest group were Koreans, and there were some Filipinos and Chinese too. Kimitsu had mixed feelings about them. He mentioned how difficult it was to look upon them as comrades, when they were strapping young men taking a lot of the remaining jobs away at a time of high day-laborer unemployment. He had nothing against them personally, indeed he said the best antidote to racism was to work alongside the Koreans and Filipinos and see that they were both nice guys and dedicated workers. But structurally, he argued, it was hard to deny that the interests of the Japanese and foreign workers were opposed. Some labor recruiters would only employ Koreans, knowing them to be fitter and harder-working than most Japanese workers, and unlikely to complain about wages and working conditions because of their illegal status. Others employed only Filipinos. Kimitsu observed that the stereotypical view of race relations in Japan, in which foreigners were an oppressed minority at the bottom of Japanese society, was being turned on its head in Kotobuki, where the foreign workers were becoming a laboring elite.

The biggest failure of my two years of fieldwork was my inability to get employed as a day laborer myself. Recruiters simply refused to take me seriously—I was an obvious foreigner who would attract the attention of the immigration office, besides which I was fat, soft, inexperienced, and had small womanish hands. But I did participate in the labor market as an employer—twice I hired Kimitsu to come and help me weed the neglected garden at my rented house in Hodogaya. After all, this too was a kind of participant observation.

On Fridays the shutters at the employment exchange would go up at 4:30 p.m., for weekend work. One Friday in April 1994 I spotted Kimitsu clinging desperately to one of the windows at the exchange in the middle of the scrum, and knew at once that he was behind with his doya rent. When the shutters went up there were hardly any jobs and none for him, so I asked him to come and help me in the garden the next day.

It was a beautiful warm sunny day. Kimitsu was due at 11 but arrived about an hour late, and by the time we'd had lunch it was 1:30 p.m. before we got started.

The garden was a very modest affair but it was a mess because I never had any time to tend to it and my wife hated gardening. We cleared sack after sack of rubbish and weeds and lumps of concrete. We had several breaks for drinks: Kimitsu's metabolism required it. When we were done, we both had showers but Kimitsu declined a change of clothing and insisted on sitting down for supper in his filthy work clothes. My wife Kazuko spread newspapers over the sofa for him to sit on and we ate at the kotatsu—a low wooden table with a heating filament underneath. It was at the end of the living room near the front door, so not as much of the room got dirty as would have happened if we had used the dining table. Kazuko was very nice to Kimitsu and gave him a slap-up meal, but she had to consider the children's environment. (That was why she'd asked me to get someone from Kotobuki in the first place—the garden had to be cleaned up for the sake of the children, and only someone used to a fairly dirty environment would take on such a job.) Kimitsu and I had orders to slash and burn and strew the scorched earth with powerful insecticides and herbicides. Kimitsu persuaded me to hold the herbicide—he said it would be a shame to kill absolutely everything in the garden. We made do with a large dose of insecticide.

Kimitsu amused my four-year-old son Jake by drawing pictures of fighter planes. He also drew a picture of me as Schindler, lifting a Nazi soldier above my head to throw him to the ground.

At this point I recognized the style, and realized with a start that Kimitsu was responsible for a lot of the graffiti around Kotobuki—I had seen numerous cartoons of SS concentration camp guards and American film stars in Nazi uniform. I should have guessed they were Kimitsu's work. He was simply projecting his personal obsessions onto the built environment.

I walked Kimitsu back to the station that evening and paid him 10,000 yen. It was slightly less than he'd get unloading rice, but on the other hand he had started work at 1:30 p.m. rather than the customary 8:30 a.m. He seemed very pleased.

He said he felt like crying when he saw my two beautiful children and my lovely house. (He didn't mention my lovely wife for some reason.) It seemed that I had everything and he had nothing. Anyway, he'd enjoyed the day's work—it made a change to do something meaningful, he said. I should call him in again, come mid-summer when the grass was up to my armpits. He'd hack his way through like Stanley going after Dr. Livingstone.

At the station we paused for a beer for me and a one-cup for Kimitsu. He didn't seem to have any change on him, so rather than make him break the 10,000 yen note I gave him 300 yen for his train fare back to Kotobuki. I realized I didn't quite know how he'd got here; the thought crossed my mind that he might even have walked the 5 miles for want of the train fare. That might account for his late arrival. One glass of saké later, he spent 200 yen of his train fare on a plastic box of strawberries for me to give to the children. In the end I just bought the ticket for him: he seemed bemused by the array of different kinds of ticket-vending machine. He wobbled unsteadily down the stairs, waving as he went.[12] It was four days after his fifty-fourth birthday, though I did not know that at the time.

One time I took Professor Arthur Stockwin, the well-known historian who was then head of the Nissan Institute of Japanese Studies at Oxford University, on a tour of Kotobuki.[13] Professor Stockwin was particularly interested in the graffiti he saw around the district: here and there someone had used a fat felt-tip pen to draw pictures of what looked to be Nazi concentration-camp guards on the walls, with various words in English and German scrawled around them. He commented that the artist appeared to be driven by some very intense obsession. "Shall I introduce you to him?" I said, and took him to Kimitsu's filthy doya room.

Again I quote my fieldnotes:

> *Kimitsu was at home in his cluttered little room, reading some heavy book as usual. He showed it to Arthur—it turned out to be a treatise on unemployment patterns in the British economy during the inter-war years. Arthur was suitably impressed.*
>
> *We went to the Hamako for a drink. Kimitsu drank three times faster than us and talked. The conversation turned to history, and Kimitsu asked Arthur if he thought Eden was really to blame for the Suez crisis.*[14] *Eden of course had opposed Chamberlain's appeasement line during the war; it was ironic that he should end up being bracketed with Chamberlain as one of the two big mess-up prime ministers. Kimitsu always thought Eden was a bit better than that. Hadn't the historians underestimated the role of the French government over Suez? Surely they had bigger interests at stake in the region than Britain?*
>
> *Arthur was visibly struggling to remember his dates and facts, but enjoying the struggle.*
>
> *By and by we were joined by Aiko, the toothless old woman who frequents the Hamako. She tried out her English on us, which consisted of just a few words, including "pochi." It turned out she meant "porch." In her youth she had worked as a cleaner for the family of an American military officer, and cleaning the porch was one of her tasks. She also had an American boyfriend*

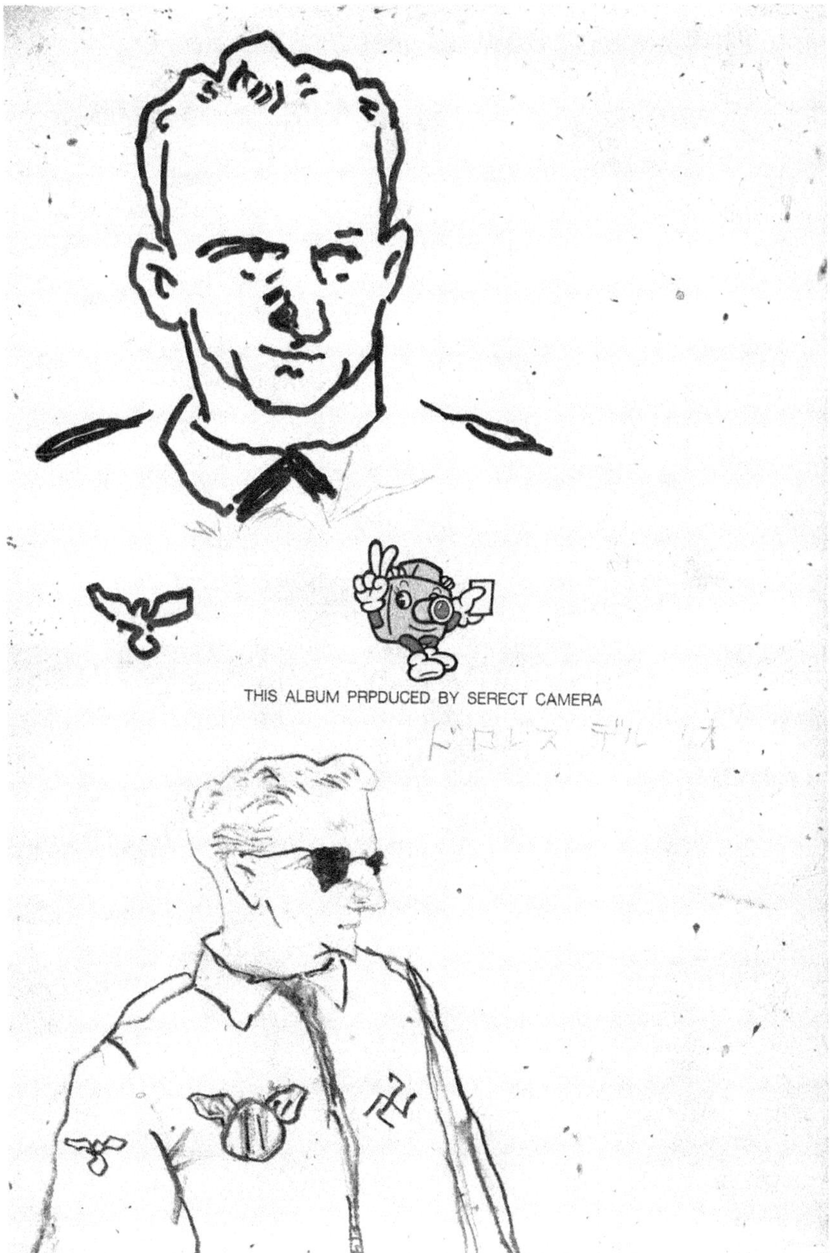

Figure 1.1. Two of Kimitsu's Nazi sketches, on the back of a cardboard photo album. In Japanese script he has written the name of Dolores del Río, the glamorous pre-war Hollywood star.

at one point, but he went back to the States and eventually dropped out of touch.

Aiko mentioned in passing that she has a part-time job at a bento shop in the Hoka-Hoka chain, which pays 610 yen an hour. It brings in 60,000 yen a month.

"She has worked hard all her life for low wages, but still she remains cheerful. Kotobuki depends on people like her," said Kimitsu.[15]

Kimitsu developed into a key informant for me, and a friend. We danced together at the Kotobuki summer festival. We hung out at bars like the Hamako and the Yuen. The Yuen had a jukebox. I usually put on *Sitting on the Dock of a Bay* by Otis Redding. Kimitsu, playfully showing off his paranoid streak, would put on *Back Stabbers*, by the O'Jays. One time I found him outside the windows of the employment exchange just as an apologetic bureaucratic voice said through the PA that there were zero jobs available. He started singing "Stay away from my window," a line from a Rod Stewart song (*Tonight's the Night*). Kimitsu was applying it satirically to the useless windows at the job center, and killing himself laughing at his own wit.

I sometimes visited his room and we talked about jazz. He'd play a few old tunes on his acoustic guitar, which was decorated with the same figures of Nazi prison guards and Jewish inmates that I'd seen on the walls of Kotobuki. He would strum along with the old jazz and rock 'n' roll songs he listened to on the American military radio station. He enjoyed the contradictions of American culture—some prim staff sergeant introducing crazy rock music by Jimi Hendrix, before solemnly warning listeners not to carry home as souvenirs any unexploded shells they might find at the firing range.

It is true I bought him quite a few drinks over the eighteen months of our acquaintanceship, but he would treat me to a drink too, when he had cash on him. I saw in the New Year (1994–1995) with him in an eerily silent bar. As a foreign researcher in a slum district I attracted a little media interest, and the two of us were photographed together in a tabloid newspaper, *Yūkan Fuji*. He also made a fleeting appearance in a late-night TV documentary about me and Kotobuki.

In sociological terms, Kimitsu was a sort of Durkheimian. He believed that human beings are weak, helpless, and swept along by forces over which they have no control: socioeconomic trends, culture, the whim of the state. Sometimes this thinking would segue into a more mystical mind-set, in which fate was the overwhelming force sweeping humans along. And in yet a third variation on this fatalistic theme, he would speculatively relate the human condition to the scientific laws governing the animal or material worlds. Hence his interest in biology, chemistry and especially physics. I decided to entitle my book *Men of Uncertainty* after hearing Kimitsu try to explain Heisenberg's uncertainty principle one morning at the Apollo Café:

> *He drew a picture of an atom on my memo pad, with an electron orbiting round the core. "We never know where the electron is," he said. "Likewise, we cannot see the future, including that of my own life. It stands on physical science, not philosophy."*[16]

The Heisenberg theory related to Kimitsu's tendency towards paranoia. Like Heisenberg's subatomic particles, we are all being influenced by unseen forces. Though he hardly ever thought ill of known individuals, Kimitsu was deeply suspicious of authorities, governments, and abstract social forces. I once found him waving his arms around and shouting "espionage" outside the labor center. A run of failures to get work had convinced him that some traitor had blacklisted him. That was paranoia at the level of everyday life. But he had a more existential sense of being controlled. Like Heisenberg's particles, human beings were unpredictable, yet subject to laws over which they had no control. Kimitsu liked Heisenberg's Uncertainty Principle as a metaphor for human life, because of its precision. The whizzing particle was uncertain, but it was not free. Likewise the uncertainty and randomness of human life should not, he argued, be mistaken for freedom. That was true of people in general, and even more so of day laborers, whose wandering lifestyle was more uncertain than those of people in regular employment, but who were still subject to the constraints of socioeconomic megatrends.

Kimitsu had been an alcoholic for many years. Most of his nutrition came from alcohol and he ate very little—though he did have an occasional hankering for raw horse meat (*basashi*). I remember him holding up his glass of cheap saké, flicking it on the side and saying "cars use gasoline, I use this." As I wrote in my book, I doubted he would live to see the new millennium.

Born in Kumamoto, on Japan's southern main island, Kyushu, Kimitsu was the second-born child, and oldest son, of four siblings. In my fieldwork I was developing a theory about oldest sons (*chōnan*). Most of the men in the doya-gai hailed from rural districts, so one would expect to find relatively few chōnan, since the oldest son is expected to inherit the household and stay on the land. In fact, however, I was noticing a surprisingly large number of chōnan among my informants. Perhaps it had something to do with rural chōnan being less equipped to cope with city life than their junior brothers, precisely because they were brought up with the expectation of staying at home before economic circumstances forced them to try their hand at migrant labor. Seasonal migrant labor has been part of rural life for hundreds of years—men, and sometimes women too, would look for work in a city during the colder months when there was little work to do on the farm. Most of them succeeded in returning to their home village in the spring. But a few did not make it. They got stuck—perhaps because they fell prey to the temptations of urban life, and got involved with gambling, women, or drinking, to the point where they were unable to send money home. For some, the shame of it all made them drop out of touch with their parental families altogether. I put it to Kimitsu that oldest sons were less likely to practice seasonal migration than junior sons, but more likely to get stuck in the city when economic circumstances forced them to do so.

When I told Kimitsu about this theory, at 6 a.m. on a cold February morning while waiting for the shutters to go up at the casual labor exchange, he thought it was spot on. He replied in English. "That's right! There are so many. Like me!" In Nishikawa English, chōnan is rendered not as "oldest son" but as "top brother"—interesting terminology, stressing relations between siblings rather than between generations.

"Something deep behind it," he said, in English. "Need careful study of Japanese traditional family system." [Peering through microscope gesture] "Must open the door." [Door-opening gesture]

> Me: oldest son stays at home, so . . .
>
> Him: "That's right. Top brother has rights. Top brother has power. So we are soft. We are spoiled. When we graduate from home . . . " [resigned shrug of shoulders.] "When I look for work, I have no . . . confidence. My whole life, I try to find why I exist. Existential . . . "
>
> Me: You've been reading Sartre and Camus.
>
> Him: Yes, and Swedenborg. Have you read Swedenborg?
>
> Me: Err . . . no. Anyway, do you understand your life now?
>
> Him: It is a punishment.
>
> Me: What for? What have you done?
>
> Him: My whole life is a punishment.
>
> Me: What for?
>
> Him: Punishment for my life! [Loud laugh]

It was 6:15. I stood back to let Nishikawa concentrate on trying to get a job. Up went the shutters—there were not as many jobs as the day before, maybe thirty or so. He surged forward with the rest. He was in the second row. I thought he ought to get one, but he wasn't pushing hard enough and others were pushing in from behind and getting their application cards in ahead of him. In a minute all the jobs were gone. But he hung on in while others were turning away in disgust, and managed to snap up a late job offer which cropped up in the hand of the clerk standing just in front of him.

He showed me the paper. "Workers, 1. Nishikawa, Kimitsu, 53, construction worker [dokō]." The job was in Mitsukyō, about 45 minutes away by foot and train. It paid 12,500 yen, plus 500 yen for lunch. "Carrying stone," he explained, gesturing lifting up paving slabs and loading them onto a wheel barrow.

"Is it a good job?"

"Hard labor! Punishment!"

He laughed loudly and said it again.

"Punishment!"

With that, he was off. I thought: He will die at sixty, in the year 2000, the last great unseen existentialist hero of the 20th century.[17]

Kimitsu also thought he would die at that age. "My old man died at the age of sixty, and I expect to do the same," he once told me. "The liver won't hold out forever. But I've no regrets. So long as you live a life that's rich and interesting, it doesn't matter whether you live to 60 or 80. Besides, salarymen don't live much past 60 either. They tire themselves out and die soon after retirement."

I gently suggested that he might prolong his life expectancy by cutting back on his drinking. "There would be no rational point whatever in trying to stop drinking, or to drink less," he said, very firmly.

The last time I saw Kimitsu in the 1990s was on the evening of Thursday March 23, 1995. It was just three days after the murderous sarin gas attack on the Tokyo subway by the Aum Shinrikyō cult—an event that made a tremendous impact on both of us (see later in this book). I stood in front of the Daimaru doya to say goodbye to Kimitsu. I said I was sorry to be leaving. He said life was full of meetings and partings; there was no point thinking too deeply about it.

"Well, I've got to go back to England and write my thesis now," I told him.

"Yeah, I'll look out for you when you get the Nobel Prize," he said.

"Unfortunately they don't give out Nobel prizes for anthropology," I pointed out.

"Maybe the Peace Prize, for bringing peace to this violent town."

"Don't be ridiculous, I haven't done Kotobuki a scrap of good."

"Yes you have!"

"So, are you going to come and see me in Britain?"

"I can already smell the roses."

"If you can just find the plane fare, I'll take care of the rest—beer included. The ticket prices have come down, you know. You can get a return ticket for 80,000 yen or less. You just have to save a little bit of money."

"Just needs one decent win on the horses!"

That was my last exchange with Kimitsu. I walked out of Kotobuki not expecting ever to see him again.

Figure 1.2. Kimitsu Nishikawa and Tom Gill, February 1994.

NOTES

1. The Kanamachi decision to join the Kobe-based Yamaguchi-gumi was a massive development in yakuza relations. It resulted in a feud between the Kanamachi and the Tokyo-based Sumiyoshi-kai. Two years later, in 2007, Kanamachi boss Kazuyoshi Kudō, whom I once interviewed, shot himself dead. See *Rokudaime Yamaguchi-gumi Kanzen Dēta Book 2008* (Comprehensive Data Book on the 6th Generation Yamaguchi-gumi), Mediabooks, 2009.

2. Field note, Monday March 7, 1994, afternoon. The English title is *The View from Afar* (1985).
3. Field note, Friday February 4, 1994, mid-afternoon.
4. Field note, Friday November 4, 1994.
5. The yen greatly fluctuated against the dollar during the period covered by this book. A very rough exchange rate would be 100 yen to the dollar.
6. Field note, Monday March 7, 1994.
7. Cf. William W. Pilcher's account of Portland longshoremen, who were systematic and ingenious in their pilfering, especially of alcohol: "The tradition of pilfering is so well established that many longshoremen feel that they have a right to pilfer and resent attempts to stop them as unjust." ("The Portland Longshoremen" in Herbert Applebaum ed., *Work in Market and Industrial Societies*, SUNY Press, 1984, p. 125). If Kimitsu's account is right, it suggests that a casual, disorganized workforce is less capable of pilfering than a regular, unionized workforce like the Portland longshoremen. The issue emerges as one of the balance of power between capital and labor.
8. Field note, Wednesday November 2, 1994, early afternoon.
9. Working 26 days or more over the previous two calendar months confers eligibility for the present calendar month.
10. Field note, Friday February 24, 1995.
11. Field note, Friday November 4, 1994.
12. Field note, Saturday April 16, 1994.
13. Field note, Saturday September 24, 1994, afternoon.
14. Anthony Eden (UK prime minister, 1955–1957) was widely blamed for the Suez crisis of 1956, when Britain made an abortive attempt to invade Egypt after President Gamal Abdel Nasser nationalized the Suez Canal.
15. Field note, Saturday September 24, 1994, afternoon.
16. Field note, Friday February 25, 1994.
17. Slightly modified from field note, Thursday February 24, 1994.

Chapter Two

Kimitsu and Kotobuki, 2004–2007

But day laborers do not die so easily. Years passed. I returned to England. I wrote my dissertation, got my doctorate, got a job as a research fellow at a small university in Kyoto, then became an associate professor at University of Tokyo and finally a professor at Meiji Gakuin University in Yokohama. One day in the autumn of 2004 I was taking a group of students on a study tour of Kotobuki when I ran into Kimitsu Nishikawa again, after an interval of nine years. His hair was running to silver but he was in excellent form and remembered me well:

"Oh, Mister Tom! Did you become a functionalist? Or a structuralist? Or are you a post-modernist these days?"

He was sixty-four. He was staying in a different doya. He had recently applied and been approved for livelihood protection, the Japanese welfare safety net (see below), so he no longer had to look for day-laboring work. He took me to his room. It was just as tiny, and just as filthy and stinking, as his old one. To be honest, I could hardly breathe in there. White cobwebs hung like silk from the ceiling, cockroaches scurried across the walls, mildew was flourishing on the lank tatami mats. And just as before, the place was littered with heavyweight books of sociology, philosophy, and religion, and old back numbers of intellectual Japanese journals like *Gendai Shisō* (Contemporary Thought), *Sekai Shisō* (World Thought), and *Risō* (Ideals). I also noticed a large number of books by the colorful Japanese thinker, Shin'ichi Nakazawa.

Kotobuki had changed more than Kimitsu had. The casual labor market had all but died. Sometimes there were no jobs at all at the casual labor exchange, and there were never more than a handful. Even the yakuza who ran the alternative labor market on the street corner had little to offer. Since the day laboring lifestyle had become unfeasible, workers with strength and ability took refuge in small construction companies that could at least guarantee regular employment. Hardly any new blood came into the *yoseba*, and that left the existing workforce stripped of its star workers and getting steadily older. The aging of the population, an issue for the whole of Japan, proceeded much more rapidly in Kotobuki. In the nine years since I'd finished my fieldwork in 1995, it had proceeded at about one year per year. In 1995 the average Kotobuki resident had been 47; now he was 56.

Many Kotobuki men had drifted into unemployment and homelessness. The local authorities had slowly and grudgingly acknowledged this fact. The obvious step would be to put the homeless men of Kotobuki on the livelihood protection (*seikatsu hogo*) program, which is the ultimate welfare safety net mandated under article 25 of the Japanese constitution, which states:

> All people shall have the right to maintain the minimum standards of wholesome and cultured living. In all spheres of life, the State shall use its endeavors for the promotion and extension of social welfare and security, and of public health.

For many years, however, local welfare officials hesitated to accept applications for livelihood protection from men in Kotobuki. There was an element of prejudice: these men were suspected of being homeless through their own laziness, and/or bad habits such as wasting money on alcohol and gambling. After all, Kotobuki had about twenty illegal gambling dens and numerous bars. But such concerns were never stated as the reason for turning away applications. Rather, the welfare office insisted that you had to have a proper residential address (*kyosho*) to apply for welfare. A homeless person living in a park or on a riverbank could not apply, and a doya room, being classified as a temporary lodging-place rather than a residence, was not acceptable either. This resulted in a Catch-22 situation: the people who most needed welfare were effectively excluded from it.

Instead of accepting livelihood protection applications from Kotobuki, the city provided a stop-gap relief program using food vouchers (officially *shokuken* but universally known as *pan-ken* or bread tickets) and lodging vouchers (*shukuhaku-ken,* but universally known as *doya-ken* or flophouse tickets). The former were worth about 700 yen and the latter, 1,500 yen. The system became heavily oversubscribed in the 1990s: 12,781 food vouchers were issued in 1990, but 346,138 in 1999. Lodging vouchers went from 10,478 in 1990 to 188,954 in 1999.[1] That is equivalent to nearly 1,000 food vouchers and 500 lodging vouchers a day.

But the lodging vouchers were not always usable—only the doya that charged 1,500 yen or less would take them, and they tended to be full. In that case, the only thing to do with the voucher was sell it to a yakuza, who would give you 500 yen for it and then use their own methods to get 1,500 yen from the city fathers for it. One did not have a room for the night, but at least one could warm up with a couple of one-cups. As for the food vouchers, they could only be used at a handful of shops, all within the Kotobuki district, and could not be used to buy alcohol or cigarettes.[2]

Another problem with this ad hoc system was that you had to stand in line every day to claim your vouchers. Since it was supposed to be no more than an emergency back-up, people were not allowed to claim for more than one day at a time. (People needing longer-term support were supposed to apply for livelihood protection—but then their application would often be turned down.) By the late 1990s, there would be hundreds of claimants waiting in line at the Naka ward office in central Yokohama every morning.

A second stop-gap response to the growing number of men lying around on the streets of Kotobuki was to set up a homeless shelter. It first opened during my fieldwork in 1994. Called the Matsukage Hostel, it was a collection of pre-fabricated buildings on a plot of land under the elevated expressway that runs above Matsukage-chō, one of the precincts adjoining Kotobuki. It was run by a large NGO called the Kanagawa-ken Kyōsaikai, which has been providing welfare services in Kanagawa-ken (the prefecture of which Yokohama is the capital city) since 1918.

But when I returned to Kotobuki in 2004, one of the biggest changes since my fieldwork in the 1990s was the appearance of a large, permanent public homeless shelter. Opened on June 1, 2003, it was an imposing seven-story building, a great white cube right in the middle of Kotobuki (figure 2.1). It is still there today. It is called *Hamakaze*, which means “beach breeze.” (The “hama” is also part of the name of the city—Yokohama. Yokohama citizens are very proud of the sea breeze that blows into the city from the beach.)

Hamakaze replaced the Matsukage Hostel and is run by the same NGO, the Kyōsaikai. It has 226 beds—206 for men, 20 on a separate floor for women—in shared rooms with four to eight beds each. That reflects the big gender imbalance in Japan’s homeless population—the women’s floor at Hamakaze has never been full.

Most of the funding to build and operate Hamakaze comes from the prefecture and the national government, which provides matching funds under the terms of the 2002 Homeless Self-Reliance Support Law. This law reflected concern over the growth in the national homeless population in the later 1990s. It had a built-in provision to lapse after ten years, but was extended for five more years in 2012 as the government was forced to admit that the homeless problem had not yet been solved.

The 2002 law created two kinds of public homeless support facility: the temporary shelter (*ichiji hinanjo*) and the self-reliance support center (*jiritsu shien sentā*). The former is a refuge for people coming straight in from the street. Homeless people are referred to them by local welfare offices or outreach teams that look for homeless people after dark. The latter is supposed to be a further rung up the ladder back to mainstream living. They

Figure 2.1. The Hamakaze Homeless Shelter in the heart of Kotobuki.

allow people to stay for a longer period while job-hunting and support them in the difficult first months after getting a job. There is considerable regional variation, but the maximum length of stay is typically one or two months at the former and four to six months at the latter.

Hamakaze was (and still is today) a hybrid institution, with the lower floors functioning as an emergency shelter and the top floor reserved for residents who have succeeded in finding a job and are building up the savings they need to make the substantial down payment required to rent a room of one's own and relaunch one's life living independently. The maximum length of stay is one month on the lower floors and six months on the upper floor. Multiple periods of residence are permitted, although one must wait at least one month before applying for readmission to the lower floors. Thus I found that some men had developed a cycle lifestyle, alternating a month in Hamakaze with a month on the streets. While in Hamakaze they would get three hot meals a day in the canteen, and a daily ration of ten cheap cigarettes—substituted with a packet of sweets for non-smokers. By 2014, the cigarette ration had been reduced to six. They were also supplied with clean clothing, wash kit, and a case worker to advise on employment, medical issues, and so forth.

Although Hamakaze provided an immediate, short-term answer to the question of where homeless people should go for the night, it was still a far cry from meeting the government's duty under article 25 of the constitution, quoted above, to guarantee "minimum standards of wholesome and cultured living." Alternating months on the street and in a bunk bed in a shelter clearly fell well short of that. Moreover, since Hamakaze, and it predecessor, the Matsukage Hostel, were in their turn the only homeless shelter in Yokohama, they had the additional effect of bringing in homeless people from other parts of the city, further accentuating Kotobuki's status as a kind of socioeconomic dumping ground.

Thus during the 1990s, as the casual labor market collapsed and the number of homeless people rose, the welfare authorities came under mounting pressure to recognize that many of the men in Kotobuki were in fact suitable candidates for the more solid welfare represented by the livelihood protection program. I will describe it in detail in chapter 4 of this book, but it basically pays about 80,000 yen a month plus rent of up to about 50,000 yen for a single person, and more if you have a family to support.

The mid-1990s brought an intense and ultimately successful campaign by a lobbying group called *Ishokujū o Hoshō Seyo! Seizonken o Kachitoru Kotobuki no Kai* (Guarantee Clothing, Food and Shelter! The Kotobuki Association for Winning the Right to Live), led by the Kotobuki Day Laborer Union (*Kotobuki-chō Hiyatoi Rōdōsha Kumiai*, or *Junichirō* for short) and supportive civil rights groups. The campaign demanded a change in the interpretation of the Livelihood Protection Law (*Seikatsu Hogo-hō*) in the city of Yokohama, to do away with the requirement for a permanent address when applying for livelihood protection.

The style of this campaign led by the Kotobuki Day Laborer Union was very dynamic. I witnessed it while I was doing fieldwork in Kotobuki in 1994. The union persuaded the local welfare authorities to engage in a series of open meetings, to which they brought large numbers of out-of-work and homeless men from Kotobuki. They hung up banners around the room, accusing the city of killing off the unemployed. They invaded the space of the city officials by hanging up banners denouncing the city's welfare policy right behind where they were sitting. They loudly harangued the officials, sometimes banging on the table and shouting in their faces. The crowd of Kotobuki men would join in vociferously.

Eventually, after a series of meetings from spring into fall, the browbeaten officials were forced to admit the need for a change of policy. It was a triumph for the union—arguably the biggest victory in the history of the modern day laborer union movement, which dates back to the oil shocks of the 1970s. It now became possible to apply for welfare without having a residential address. That is as it should be, since article 19 of the Livelihood Protection Law (*Seikatsu Hogo-hō*) clearly states that an address is not required to apply for livelihood protection. One needs a residential address to start *receiving* welfare payments (*seikatsu hogo kaishi*)—not to *apply* for them in the first place (*seikatsu hogo shinsei*). The insistence on a residential address when applying was a typical example of local policy implementation that deliberately circumvented the letter of the law—a common problem in Japan.

The relaxing of the welfare policy came at the same time that day-laboring jobs were drying up in the wake of the bursting of the bubble economy at the start of the 1990s. These two factors between them led to a drastic increase in the number of welfare recipients in Kotobuki. In 1991 there were 2,291 people living on livelihood protection in a total doya population of 6,334. By 1998, there were 5,274 livelihood protection recipients in a doya population of 6,495.[3] Thus by the turn of millennium, over 80% of the rooms in the doya were occupied by people receiving livelihood protection.

This was the reform that enabled Kimitsu to go on welfare. When I first knew him, in 1993, he had no expectation of being looked after by the welfare authorities. He viewed himself and his fellow day laborers as "disposable labor" (*tsukaisute rōdō*), to be used when convenient, then left to die on the street once they were no longer able to contribute labor to the longshoring and construction industries. But the city of Yokohama had softened, and now, for most people there, the constitutional promise of basic standard of living for all citizens was finally being kept—at least for those over the age of sixty. Although the age limit is not stated in the Japanese Livelihood Protection Law any more than the address rule was, officials are still reluctant to accept welfare applications from people—especially men—under the age of sixty.

That ad hoc provision is a tough one for Kotobuki men, since hard work and hard living tends to make them age more rapidly than other men. They have to somehow survive to the age of sixty to escape from spells of homelessness and life eked out with dwindling day-laboring opportunities, informal economy activities like can and magazine recycling, and standing in line for food and accommodation vouchers.

Like his fellow day laborers, Kimitsu had a hard time at the end of the 1990s—he struggled to get more than a few days' work in a month, but somehow he managed to hang on to his doya room—and his books. A spell of homelessness would have made it very difficult to keep his library intact. But shortly after his sixieth birthday in April 2000, he made a successful application for livelihood protection and he has been living on it ever since.

Having renewed our acquaintance, I started going out drinking with Kimitsu again, listening to him talk about stuff. As the year 2007 dawned, he was going on sixty-seven. He was surprisingly healthy for one who had lived on alcohol for so long—he seemed to eat almost nothing—but he could not defy old age and death forever. I loved listening to him talk, but it seemed a shame that I was the only one listening. I was reminded of the singer Laurie Anderson who once said that when her father died, it was as if a whole library had burned down.[4] One day, I mused, Kimitsu Nishikawa is going to die . . . and a great big library is going to go down in flames. So I decided to try and write down the essentials of his life and thoughts before it was too late.

For half a year, I took him to one of our old haunts, the Apollo café, a couple of times a month, with an old laptop computer of mine that lived in Kimitsu's doya room. The Apollo café was a cavernous, dimly lit coffee shop run by a couple of Korean women. It smelled of damp carpet and stale cigarette smoke, but it was quiet and there was a socket to plug in the computer. I would lay the computer down on an electronic poker game table between us. I would order a coffee, Kimitsu would order a glass of shōchū, of course, and then he would rap for two or three hours while I desperately tried to keep up with the task of writing it down on the computer. I did it all in Japanese, and what follows is my own English translation of the transcript.

Kimitsu dropped a lot of names in his discourse; some of them I had not heard of. I would go home clutching a floppy disc with the day's notes on it, transfer the data to my home computer, and then surf around the net for information on the thinkers and writers that Kimitsu liked to discuss. I suppose it was slightly embarrassing—a university professor with less book-learning than a retired day laborer. But it was an education. I did my best to catch up, and would come back the next week armed with questions on the previous week's topic. I would print out the notes and give them to Kimitsu to read. He made quite a few corrections.

I deliberately kept my own part in the conversation to a minimum, occasionally asking a question or making a brief comment to prompt Kimitsu to get going again. I wanted to be Boswell to his Johnson. I knew he liked that idea, being a big fan of Doctor Johnson. I edited the notes only lightly. Kimitsu would mingle talk about his life with reflections on politics, philosophy, quantum mechanics, and so on. For the most part I did not attempt to separate the strands out. I left them mingled together so that the reader could share the experience of listening to Kimitsu's rambling discussions. In Japan there is a tradition of this kind of thing—a *zatsudan*, or "miscellaneous discussion."

Sometimes I also brought along a sketch pad so that Kimitsu could illustrate his discussion. As well as being an intriguing conversationalist, he also has a certain artistic flair, although all the people he sketches—politicians, baseball players, movie stars—tend to look oddly similar to the Nazi concentration camp guards he used to draw on the walls of Kotobuki.

Sometimes Kimitsu would start talking in his self-taught English. I have left those passages the way he said them, and italicized them. I have also italicized my own comments and questions.

Kimitsu Nishikawa—overlooked genius? Or just an eccentric old drunkard? Have a read and see what you think.

NOTES

1. Gill, *Men of Uncertainty*, p. 211.
2. Starting in 2002, a volunteer support group called *Sanagitachi* ('Chrysalises') started offering three hot meals a day in exchange for a food voucher. That service continues to this day.
3. Gill, *Men of Uncertainty*, p. 202.
4. Laurie Anderson, "World Without End." From the album *Bright Red* (1994).

Chapter Three

The 2007 Conversations

The First Conversation

February 3, 2007

My name is Kimitsu Nishikawa. I was born in Kumamoto city in 1940, the 15th year of the Showa era. Others born in that year include John Lennon, Al Pacino, Peter Frampton, Raquel Welch, Jack Nicklaus and the great sumo champion, Taihō.

My parents gave me a very pompous name. They called me "Norimitsu" (紀光), meaning something like, "light of the century." That's my formal name in the family registry. Those were nationalistic times—1940 was celebrated as the 2600th anniversary of the founding of the nation by emperor Jimmu, and the "nori" in Norimitsu is also the final character of the *Nihon Shoki*, or Chronicles of Japan (日本書紀), which were compiled in the 8th century and supposed to have all the history about Jimmu and how he was the direct descendent of the sun goddess Amaterasu. It was a dark age. I never liked my name. When I was young, a fortune teller told me it was an unlucky name, because the character *kawa* (川) in Nishikawa had three strokes and the character *nori* (紀) in Norimitsu had nine strokes, and three plus nine equals twelve, which signifies a bad life, easily getting neurotic, likely to have difficulty in getting married, etc., etc.

The *nishi* (西) in Nishikawa is a problem too. It means "west," and in Buddhist cosmology all bad things come from the west. The realm of the dead is always in the west. In English "gone west" means somebody died, right? The Dalai Lama's looked into this, you know, and I too am interested in this kind of thing. It's a strange dialectic. Does the cosmos itself undoubtedly exist? That's a pretty crazy question. G. K. Chesterton looked into it too, in his own way, with that characteristic humor of his. I reckon that's why

Chesterton has been so popular in the Orient. His discussion on the death penalty is interesting. He writes somewhere, "If you are opposed to the death penalty, don't hang around screaming about it outside the prison—get into the prison, embrace the man who is due to be hanged, shed all your tears and say "you should not have to die!"[1] In other words he was an empiricist. In the sense that he paid attention to individual human beings rather than the generality.

I got interested in Chesterton when I was working at the docks. Somehow his name cropped up a few times on the Pete Smith show on FEN,[2] and I thought I'd like to read this guy. I'd read the Father Brown detective stories when I was a kid, but this time I started reading his criticism, and I was surprised. His use of analogy, allegory and exemplar is just incredible. He'll make you laugh—but he'll also persuade you. I really do recommend Chesterton's criticism.

Now that I've passed the age of 65, more and more of my friends are dying off. Muto-kun's died, and Hayashi-kun.[3] My own kid brother got run over and killed at 62. So it's only natural that I've recently started to feel like going home.

Home to me is Yamaga, in Kumamoto prefecture, Kyushu. I was born in Kumamoto city, but I was evacuated to Yamaga because of the war. It's a small town on a plain in the middle of the mountains—known as the hometown of Shinichi Etō, who played baseball for the Chūnichi Dragons, and Noboru Kōzuki, the Takarazuka[4] star. The present minister of agriculture, Toshikatsu Matsuoka-chan,[5] is from those parts too. I know he doesn't have a very clean reputation, but still, he's done well to become such an influential man. I really like him actually, because he's got a Yamaga kind of character. He's a country boy. He's clumsy. He always seems like he's his own worst enemy. Maybe he does a few naughty things, but then, all politicians do. He's bad at getting along in the world. When country boys go to the big city, they have to get a lot better at cheating to get by.[6] There are a lot of eccentric politicians from northern Kyushu. Like Taku Yamasaki[7] and Fumio Kyūma.[8] Kyūma really enjoys bashing the Americans, eh? But he's smiling while he says those things, so you can't hate the guy. He just says what he thinks—straight. OK, he's a bit stupid. The kind of guy who'll drink water while he's drowning. I think there's a place in this world for guys like him, no?

The other day I made a trip back to Yamaga. After I turned 65, I suddenly started thinking about my hometown, and since then I've been back about five times. I drink too much, and death is catching up on me now, so it occurred to me that I should go back to my home country one time, see my big sister, see the old mountain peaks of my youth, get a look at that beautiful countryside. Then I could go back to Yokohama and die in peace. It wouldn't do to die without seeing those places again. I felt like o-Jizō-sama[9] and a few other little gods were telling me "hey you—go home one time." Call it a whim. A momentary impulse. If an impulse like that comes to you, well—you've just got to obey it, right? But I took care to get my personal seal and documents from my room before I set out. I wasn't too impulsive to look after my valuables.

It's quite an operation, getting back to Kyushu from here. It's about 500 miles. I used a special way of travelling I call the "gun" (*teppō*). It means buying a cheap ticket and then using it to fly a long distance like a bullet from a gun.

I bought a ticket for a couple of hundred yen at Ishikawachō station. I got about as far as Shizuoka with that, on a stopping train.[10] Then I chose a little unmanned station and got off there. There was no one around so I slept on the platform. Then I bought some saké from a vending machine, bought myself another 200 yen ticket, and this time I got as far as Toyohashi. I told the ticket collector there that I'd got drunk and lost my ticket, and managed to carry on as far as some little unmanned station in Gifu prefecture, where I spent the night and then bought another little ticket. This time I got as far as Osaka. I told them I was from Nishinari,[11] and that I'd fallen asleep and missed my stop at Takatsuki, had a few drinks and lost my ticket. There are lots of people like that in Osaka, so they'll believe you right away.

Then I got on a bus for Nanba and headed for Kamagasaki. What a great place that is. I lived there for a year or so, ages ago. It's got a more at-home atmosphere than Kotobuki. Everyone there is from western Japan, including a lot from Kyushu. We Kyushu guys know each other right away. "You're from Kumamoto, right?" That kind of thing.

When were you living in Kamagasaki?

Just after I left senior high school, before I went into the Ground Self Defense Force.[12] Osaka has a pretty bad image, which it kind of deserves. I was working as a plumber, and I hated the work and the company that employed me. I like rough-and-ready jobs. Like carrying bananas. Plumbing is a fiddly job—can't stand it. I quit in about six months. But Nanba[13] was good. Plenty of cinemas and *monjayaki*.[14] The three great skid rows of Japan—Kamagasaki, Kotobuki and San'ya in Tokyo—are all roughly the same, but Kamagasaki is run by the Yamaguchi-gumi,[15] so the atmosphere is slightly different. The Kamagasaki yakuza are scary. They'll kill people for some silly little thing. I knew this country boy who'd come down to Kamagasaki all the way from Aomori, and he just carelessly brushed against the shoulder of some yakuza and he was beaten to death. His body was chucked into the Dōtonbori River. Osaka people will do stuff like that quite casually. But they do have their kind side too. The concierge at the flophouse where I was staying used to make curried rice for me when I got home from work.

As you were saying before I interrupted . . .

Riding the gun. When the ticket inspector comes along, you just go to the toilet, or start coughing violently or making like you're about to throw up, so that the inspector doesn't want to get too close to you. You don't want to ride the gun in a suit and necktie. But with this kind of blue worker's overalls, you're generally OK. One time, though, I did run out of luck at Sagamihara, and had seven thousand yen taken off me. I had tried to get on an express train—that's where I blew it. Plus I was sober. It's no good being sober. So long as you're good and drunk, the ticket inspector doesn't come near you. Call it the mysterious power of alcohol, if you like.

At Nishinari I usually spend a few nights roughing it, sleeping in Triangle Park[16] or around Nanba station. But this time I didn't stay—just got back on the train. I got as far as Himeji and slept one night in front of the station. Then I got another 200 yen ticket which got me all the way to Kyushu. I got off the train several times on the way, and watched what the station staff were doing while I waited for the next train. Anyway, the whole point of riding the gun is to avoid paying a substantial fare. There's no fun in paying out big fares, right? Because your adversary is the representative of authority—and you have to resist authority.

I got off at Kumamoto. There is no train to Yamaga. There used to be, back in the day, but Kyushu has a whole lot of typhoons and landslides and the railway line got so messed up that they just couldn't make a going concern out of it. So I just got on the bus and did the last 35 kilometers to Yamaga without using the gun. It took about an hour.

It was my first visit to Yamaga for 30 years, and the place had changed quite a bit. But the fundamental character of the place hadn't changed. There'd been no revolution. They hadn't suddenly achieved enlightenment down there. It was just that my sister had got older, and a lot of my old buddies had died. The landscape had changed a bit, but the river was still running. The familiar peak of the Fudōiwa[17] was still there.

I went to look at my old high school. I kept thinking of that poem by Charles Lamb, "The Old Familiar Faces": "Ghost-like I paced round the haunts of my childhood . . . Seeking to find the old familiar faces . . . All, all are gone, the old familiar faces."[18] Lamb also went back to his school after several decades. And there was no one he knew in the grounds of the school. I was very moved when I read that poem. It was the same for me. In the old days I had lots of friends, but now I couldn't find one. Of course I couldn't. I first read that poem of Lamb's a long time ago, and I always thought it was a terrific work of nostalgia. I've always thought it has a Buddhist scent to it.

Yamaga itself really is a ghost town. It feels just like a movie set: the townscape is there, but there are no people. It's a hot-spring town, in the volcano zone. In the old days they had this giant bath, called the "Thousand Person Bath"—admission was 2 yen. For 5 yen you could use the bath in one of the inns or a public bath. There were lots of people there, children running around all over the place, young men and women flirting with each other. But now there's nobody there. You'd not be surprised if a few ghosts showed up. It's a zombie town. Why do politicians let this kind of thing happen, I wonder? Do they reckon that little rural villages just don't matter? Since you can import your agricultural produce from America. And your timber from Indonesia. Just use the country for golf courses.

Apart from my sister and her son, there wasn't a single person there that I knew. I went to the houses of several old friends and knocked on the door, but nobody came out. I didn't have much time, so I didn't hang around for long. It would have been nice if I'd had the time and money to make like Ernest Hemmingway, checking into a hotel for a month or so and smoking a few cigars while I checked out the neighborhood, but I had to ride the gun back home pretty soon and it was on my mind. I think at least one of them was in when I knocked, but he didn't come to the door. In other words they were like dead people, like mummies. And besides, I wasn't some hotshot intellectual like Claude Lévi-Strauss—just a traveler who rides the gun. That place felt like a foreign country. I'd rather be in Kotobuki. At least this town is still alive. Down in Yamaga you never know what kind of zombie might suddenly come out from somewhere.

My sister is a widow, and she lives with her son. Her husband died four or five years ago. Her son's over thirty now, and he does various odd jobs around Kumamoto, working as a plumber or carpenter, but he still lives with his mother.

First I called from the phone at the public hot-spring bath. She was kind enough to send a taxi for me. When I got there it was already 11 o'clock at night. I would have got there earlier, but it felt so nostalgic being back in Kumamoto that I'm afraid I had a few drinks. When I arrived, my sister and nephew came out to meet me carrying torches. "Welcome," she said. It did feel good. But that was the last I saw of my nephew—he went straight upstairs and never came back down. Not that I think he's a bad person. I was in the wrong—suddenly showing up like that looking like a tramp, and in the middle of the night too.

I gave them some crackers I'd bought in Kumamoto.[19] And I had a little chat with my sister. I told her about my feelings. That I wanted to talk to her one more time before I died, that I wanted a little talk that I could take home like a souvenir, and that I wanted to see the mountains. I said some superficial things. How fantastic it was that she had become headmistress of a kindergarten, how great that she'd built herself a fine house—that kind of thing. To me, my sister is like Queen Himiko.[20] I didn't go into much detail about myself. She already knows perfectly well that I'm a loser. She asked me how I'd managed to pay the fare all the way from Yokohama, so I told her I'd ridden the gun. She didn't understand what that meant, so I had to explain. In the end we spoke for three or four hours. Then she laid out a futon for me. The next morning, I went home. She gave me 50,000 yen. "I don't suppose you've got any money," she said. We hated each other when we were high school kids, but she looked after me very well.

The first time I rode the gun down to Yamaga was in July of the year before last, for *Obon*.[21] This one I just came back from was the fifth, and I've visited my sister on about three of those occasions. I always show up without warning, and she's always kind to me, but this time she said "the neighbors are gossiping about this strange-looking man who comes to my house, so please don't come anymore." I said, "OK, I've got it. I'll be off, then," and then I pushed off.

It's tough, you know—riding the gun. If they spot you, all you can do is run away—which I can't really do, now that I'm past 65. I don't have the energy for it anymore, so I guess I probably won't do it again.

The Second Conversation

February 17, 2007

Three days ago, I'd had a few drinks and was walking through Chinatown, when three Chinese guys came up and asked me for directions to the Kanteibyō temple. While I was explaining, they came quite close and sort of jostled up against me, and when I got back to my room I found that my wallet was gone. To be honest those guys looked pretty shady and I should have been on my guard, but I have no evidence that they took the wallet. I could have just dropped it on my way home. It was my own fault. It was a good lesson, really. I had 5,000 yen back in my room, and I've been getting by with that ever since. I've been curled up at home the last three days. I've not been out once and I haven't even had a drink. Today I finally bought me a glass of the cheapest saké.

I lent Kimitsu 10,000 yen, and asked him to tell me about his childhood.

I was born in Kumamoto city, Kumamoto prefecture. I only have gestalt-like memories of my early days. In 1940, the year I was born, the war was in full swing. It was an age of extremes. Sadaharu Ō[22] was born that year you know. Why did America join in the war in Europe, I wonder? True, if they hadn't, Europe would probably have become one huge graveyard.

My earliest memory is from when I was three. I could see the railway tracks on the far side of the Tsuboi River. It was part of the national railways. There were steam trains running along it, and I enjoyed wondering where on earth they might be going. I don't remember this next bit myself, but according to my sister and a few others, I got lost one time, walking along the tracks. The police and the fire brigade were all out looking for me, apparently. I haven't the slightest memory of doing any such thing myself, but it is true that I was an inquisitive little boy. I loved travelling even when I was very small. Later I'd go out looking for grasshoppers and stag beetles. I'd walked quite a way by the time they found me, I'm told. Maybe I had some kind of latent interest in travel.

One day there was a fire on the far side of the river. There were flames coming out of somebody's house—I was surprised, indeed shocked. To think that something as solid and certain as a house could disappear, just like that. I saw it, and I thought, "no good will come of staying in a house. Better to keep on the move." I was only three, and it was still peaceful then.

One day, when I was on my way home from the public bath with my mother, I saw an enormous tank. It was making a terrific noise. I thought "if we've got terrible things like this, maybe we can beat America."

When I was four or five, we evacuated from Kumamoto to Yamaga. It happened very suddenly. I didn't have time to express an opinion. I was only a kid, so my opinion didn't count anyway. A truck came, and we put all our stuff on it. "You—hop on board." Like that. "Is it really OK to do things so suddenly?" I wondered. Well, I could hear the sound of falling bombs occasionally, so it was only natural to evacuate from the city to the country. I guess it was 1945, and the American air-raids were gradually getting more intense. In April there was a big raid on Kumamoto city and about 500 people were killed. So it's just as well we evacuated to Yamaga. My father made the right decision there. My father was very smart (*Kimitsu sheds a tear*). I want to be like my father. There's a lake near Kumamoto called Lake Ezu. My dad used to go boating there, and he looked very dashing. He was good at running the marathon too. A sporting person. He'd graduated from Chinsei high school. It's a private school with a right-wing, Spartan kind of education, like Kokushikan in Tokyo. He was a banker. He managed to get into Yasuda Bank with a leg-up from his own dad.

Yasuda was an old samurai bank. My father's father was a bit of a, how should I put it, a bit of a yakuza-type guy, or a bit of a rural samurai, born in the Edo era. He always wore a *hakama*. That helped us quite a bit. After all, in those days all the men were being sent off to the war. This was an age where you'd be arrested and killed right away if you just said you were against the war.

My mother was the daughter of a wealthy landlord who practiced large-scale agriculture. A model farmer. But she lost contact with her family after her marriage. Her older sister married into a farming family, but died of tuberculosis around the age of 35. This was before the War, when agriculture was mostly done by hand. It was a tough way of life, even for relatively wealthy families. You don't want to go into farming. They lost touch during the war. The family physically collapsed.

About 1972, my father died. He was 62. I was about 32, I suppose. He died young, from stress and booze. He was in Kumamoto University Hospital at the end. Since I was his eldest son, I took a month off dock work and went down to Kumamoto to look after him. But I couldn't look after him indefinitely. I wanted to get back to work, and I wanted to have a drink. So I told my mother I was awfully sorry, but it was bye-bye time.

When I was looking after my father in hospital, I would buy whisky with my pocket money. I hid it in my pocket. One day my mother found out, and she got very angry with me. I took a slap in the face there. She threw the bottle away and smashed it. "Here's your dad in a serious condition and you're boozing in the hospital!" So I thought, "maybe I'll head off back to Yokohama by and by." Because I did want to have a drink. So I got permission from my mother to leave Kumamoto University Hospital and I went back to Yokohama. He died a month later. My father liked a drink and he drank every day, but that wasn't the cause of death. It was cancer. A karmatic disease. It was the war that messed everything up. I rather think that the stress of the war messed up my father. He was always running away, and I think that became very stressful for him.

I think we're seeing a regression phenomenon among humans today. People run away from the truth. The worst of all is the authorities, the state. Thanks to the state all sorts of absurd, irrational things have cropped up. That was the biggest theme of the twentieth century. We just couldn't live in a relaxed, calm sort of way anymore. Even now we don't know when North Korea might drop an atomic bomb on Japan. It's an uneasy, Franz Kafka kind of feeling. Kafka was lucky he died before Hitler took power.

I'm not good at talking about my mother. I was effectively separated from her from the age of three. We were still living in the same house, but my relationship with my mother gradually got weaker. Like being weaned from the breast, sort of thing. It's the same in Europe, right? Role playing, division of labor. I was brought up by my grandparents. My mother was busy with the housework and shopping, so she didn't have much time for us kids. I spent a lot of time with my grandparents. I was brought up by them, mainly. They meant a lot to me, my granddad and grandma. In families these days the grandparents nearly always live separately, right? That's all wrong. You can't receive the wisdom of the senior generation. In my case I was very lucky to have my grandfather with me.

I cannot say that what my seniors (the generation that fought the Pacific War) did was good. But now things are scarier. They'll kill people quite casually these days. I think we need a new style of thought.

My grandfather didn't last long before he died though. He was a right-wing person and very patriotic, so he was deeply affected by defeat in the war. After we lost the war, he walked all the way from Kumamoto to our house in Yamaga. He had a walking stick, and he carried all his luggage on his back. He was all messed up, and crying out for help. But he died about three days later. I think he was worn out by the war. My grandfather and my father both had short lives. Call it fate, or DNA. Ronald Reagan lived to be 93. Charles Bronson lived to be 81. We don't have that kind of vitality in my family. Or is it just that having money makes you live a long life? J.K. Galbraith lived past the age of 90 too.

When my grandfather arrived at our house, my mother didn't look particularly pleased to see him. She gave him a very funny look. Maybe she was bothered because we didn't have any food and he was another mouth to feed. But it was such a funny look she gave him that I think there may have been more to it than that. It was a mysterious face. The moment I saw it I thought "uh-oh, I don't like the look of this. Something might happen here." That's a child's intuition for you. Something about the atmosphere. (*Into English*) "Looks nasty"—(*Back to Japanese*) that's what I thought. At the time, my grandmother was already gone. She'd died during the war, I think. My grandfather didn't have any particular wounds on him, and I think he died from the feeling that he was in the way. A feeling that he was making trouble for those around him. It would have been better if he'd stayed in Kumamoto and gone begging around the American military base.

At the time there were three of us kids, and a fourth on the way. We really had nothing to eat. So it is a fact that granddad was in the way. "So, you went and survived the war, eh?"—that was the feeling. He wasn't any use, he just ate food. Just like the way I am these days. There's a Buddhist saying: "Demons go and disappear somewhere where they can't be seen by human eye."[23] That's what the family wished he'd done, truth to tell. Just quietly disappear.

That was my golden age, when I was living in Kumamoto and Yamaga up to the age of five. My dad was a banker, and I had my granddad and grandma to bring me up. The American bombing raids hadn't started yet. I walked 2,000 meters along the railway track to the next station. At the age of 3 and all. I guess I had the DNA of a rambling man.

The people who've had the biggest influence on me are the likes of Guru Nakazawa[24] and Colin Wilson.[25] Then there's Herman Hesse, John Steinbeck, Somerset Maugham, and Dostoevsky's writings from prison in Siberia.[26] Quite a mixed bag, isn't it? There's no consistency—because I have no education.

(I pointed out that there was only one Japanese in his list of heroes.)

There are Japanese people I admire. My father. Guru Nakazawa. Particularly excellent foremen down on the docks. Heroes whose names I don't know.

They are real heroes. But I do also have a soft spot for Anthony Eden and Edward Heath. Eden was a very dashing man, don't you think? He always looked so smart you'd not have been surprised to see him modelling for Saville Row, and Heath was a great musician. I also like men who've done battle with the sea, like Francis Chichester[27] and Robin Knox-Johnston.[28] There are a lot of Englishmen among my heroes.

Guru Nakazawa took a lot of heat over the Aum Shinrikyō problem, but I think any scholar should be allowed to make one or two mistakes. Paul Kammerer got so heavily criticized by William Bateson that he committed suicide.[29] George Orwell,[30] Arthur Koestler[31] —they've been heavily criticized too. Guru Nakazawa is an enthusiastic scholar. Look how many books he's published. And he's an empiricist. He's got a lot of detailed knowledge about myth. I reckon his key works are *The Mozart of Tibet*, *Lenin for Beginners*, *Barcelona*, *The Sacred Number 3*, and *Green Capitalism*. Those books constitute the core of his work, I'd say. And the key elements in his thought would be symmetry, oppression, and knowledge—latent, unconscious, flexible knowledge.

When Nakazawa talks about symmetry,[32] he means that if you observe from a great distance, the differences between people, or between people and animals or plants, do not seem particularly significant. Humans are not a particularly outstanding thing. That's the kind of amusing viewpoint you get with Nakazawa. He spent three years in Tibet, so he does have a certain persuasive power. I envy him. I'd love to go to Tibet, but since I'm broke I can't buy the air ticket. When I was young—about 19—I saw this feature about Tibet in *Asahi Graph* magazine. There were photos of the Dalai Lama and the Panchen Lama. I didn't tell anyone, but from that moment I was in love with Tibet. I think it's wonderful that Nakazawa really went there. What a feeling! Like a baseball player sliding in to home base head-first to score the winning run. I think Guru Nakazawa may be the reincarnation of one of the great Tibetan lamas of the past.

The Third Conversation

February 25, 2007

I well remember the day the war ended. That day, there was the bluest sky I've ever seen. It really moved me, as a kid. It was incredibly quiet. You could have heard a pin drop. And the sky was blue. Pure blue. We didn't have the kind of atmospheric pollution you get nowadays. There were no American bombers. All thanks to the war ending. The present generation—baby boomers, Tetsuya Takeda's generation[33] —I bet they've never seen a sky that blue. Because that generation was born in the midst of environmental destruction. That's the pollution generation. The contaminated generation.

I pity them. I myself am from the inflated expense-claim, post-Auschwitz generation.

I didn't hear the Emperor's surrender broadcast, but I read it later in a weekly magazine. In those days magazines consisted almost entirely of war photographs. A brilliant attack by the German Panzers and so on. *Asahi Graph* was full of German propaganda. Later, when I went to high school, I learned about Auschwitz for the first time in the pages of the *Sunday Mainichi*.

Before the war, my father owned a 9.5 millimeter projector. It was made by the French company, Pathé, and he had a few films, slapstick comedies with Charlie Chaplin, that kind of thing. He would put on film nights for the neighbors. In those days there were still lots of houses that didn't even have a radio, so this was fantastic. We also watched newsreels. We'd see German soldiers riding on Panzer tanks as they took over Europe. In these propaganda movies the German soldiers were always great big blond guys. After the war, a lot of American soldiers came to Kumamoto, and a lot of them were big blond guys as well. I was only five, so I didn't understand the difference between German soldiers and American soldiers. To me it was like these blond supermen who conquered Europe had now come and conquered Japan.

Compared with the war years, my parents finally showed some relief in their faces. At last the family was at peace, and the tension relaxed. Those were good times. Although there were a few fights among us children. Since my dad lost his job at the bank, he'd been working for the Food Corporation—the public body in charge of distributing rations. When he quit the bank, he got drunk (which very rarely happened) and got into a row with my mother. She criticized him for quitting the bank.[34]

When the war ended, I was five years old and attending kindergarten. I hated kindergarten. I was bullied by one of the older kids. I can still remember his name: Toyoda-kun. If I ever meet him again, I'd like to give him a good beating. Then I went to elementary school. I hated that too, except for the first year, which wasn't too bad. We had the same textbooks that they used during the war, but all the really patriotic bits had been deleted with black ink. Nearly all the teachers were just back from the army, and they were very violent. Yasunobu Kawahara sensei, for instance. Just a tiny bit of chatting in class and he'd give you a stinging slap. It felt like prison. He'd pull the girls' hair too. "That is wrong!" he'd say as he punished you. But he was the one doing wrong. Before you punish someone you have to explain why whatever they did was wrong. The elementary school was a postwar battlefield.

I hate authority. Authoritarian teachers, priests, and so on. Christ or Buddha would never have behaved the way they do. Real gods are not authoritarian.

I did have some good friends though. And when I was in 4th and 5th grade, there was a very pretty girl sitting next to me, who went on to become an actress in the famous Takarazuka theatre. Kimiko Haraguchi. Her father ran a shop that sold cameras and stationery, and she brought in quite a few customers for him with her looks. Her big sister won a beauty contest and got to be Miss Kyushu. When Kimiko took up acting, she used the stage-name Noboru Kōzuki. She didn't have much education, so she spelled her own name wrong. She meant to use the kanji for "rising up" (昇; usually pronounced "Noboru"), but she wrote it with the kanji for "bright" (晃; which is usually pronounced "Akira").

Figure 3.1. Photos of Noboru Kōzuki from Kimitsu's album (Cuttings from weekly magazines).

She really set my heart pounding. I used to peep at her from behind my schoolbooks. Furtively . . . since it wouldn't have done to be spotted by that sadistic teacher. It was entirely unrequited love, alas.

My worst subject was mathematics. Especially those problems with words, where you're supposed to apply mathematical principles to real-life situations. If it was just numbers, I could just about get by. My best subject was Japanese. I loved writing the complex characters, just as I loved drawing. Sometimes we went outdoors to do sketching, but then I would dash off some crappy sketch as quick as I could, and use the spare time to laze around with my friends, going to the sweet shop to buy lemonade and so on. We'd all pool our money. I do like fieldwork.

But on the whole, elementary school was hell for me. And not just me. Everybody looked bored out of their heads. It's the same all over the world, isn't it? The poet Shuntarō Tanikawa[35] never went to school at all, you know. He was the son of a wealthy family, and he just occasionally dropped in at a sort of temple school when he felt like it. The school system itself is all wrong—we should ditch it.

Middle school was a bit more fun than elementary school. I went to Yamaga middle school. I read various books and raised my consciousness a little. I played various amusing games with my friends. I did get into fights though, occasionally. There were some mild-mannered teachers, intellectual teachers, teachers who hadn't been in the army. Even some slightly avant-garde teachers. It helped that a little more time had passed since the end of the war. My grades were middling—I'd be about tenth in my class. But my part-time job took up a lot of my time. I delivered newspapers. I had to collect the money too.

I did get to see a lot of movies. Yamaga was only a little town but it had two cinemas—Daiei and Shōchiku. The Daiei cinema showed movies by the likes of Paramount, Columbia and Rank. At Shōchiku they showed films from Metro Goldwyn Meyer, Warner Brothers, Twentieth Century Fox, Tōei etc. I saw *Mito Kōmon*[36] there. The cinemas would ask us to fold their fliers into the newspaper, and they'd give us free tickets in exchange. MGM was always coming out with these over-the-top films, like *Ben Hur*. I got three tickets a month from each cinema, so I could watch six movies a month. Though I wasn't supposed to—cinemas were frowned upon by the school authorities. One day I noticed one of my teachers sitting very near me. Damn! Was he going to slap me? But it was all right. He kindly pretended not to notice me. Going to the movies so often, I got to like a lot of film stars. Trevor Howard, James Mason, Wilfred Hyde-White, Marilyn Monroe, Christopher Lee, Peter Cushing.

The Korean War was really interesting and funny.[37] Every day there'd be articles about it in the newspapers and magazines, and photos too. I pinned them to the wall in my room and was always poring over them. One day the northern forces would be sweeping into the south; another day the south would be striking back. War really is interesting, you know, so long as the bombs aren't falling on your own town.

Then I had to sit the exam for high school. [In English] *It's a very special test.* I wrote on the palm of my hand, but it was only art. I wasn't trying to cheat. Noboru Kōzuki was there in the examination hall, so that cheered me up. I wondered if she was at all interested in me, and thought how nice it would be if we ended up going to the same high school . . . I passed. Of course she was still using her real name in those days. Kimiko Haraguchi. She became famous. But she died eight years ago, at the age of 58. After she passed 50 I started to notice the stress in her face. Intestinal cancer, it was.

What year was it?

1999. March 25. In the early evening.

I went to Yamaga High School. I was surrounded by beauties. It was incredible. You know—the hormones. I became more enthusiastic about the newspaper delivering, especially collecting the money. Because sometimes I could get a glimpse of some of those beauties in their home setting while I was collecting the money. Usually the mother would do the paying, but sometimes I'd catch a glimpse of her daughter standing behind her, and I'd blush like crazy—my face would be bright red. When I went to Noboru Kōzuki-kun's house, or Hideko Hara's house, or Yoshimoto-kun's, the chemist's daughter. It was hopeless. I knew I'd be in trouble if one of these mothers caught me giving her daughter the eye, so I felt a bit ambivalent about the whole thing.

I never had a girlfriend in high school. Well, if I were to stretch a point I might mention Noboru Kōzuki. She wasn't my girlfriend though—it was just unrequited love. But we did go around together a bit. Of course I didn't call her *kun*[38] in those days—that was only after she started playing male roles at Takarazuka. She wasn't a lesbian or anything. She was all woman. I also used to hang out with Yoko Watanabe,[39] the bicycle shopkeeper's daughter. She had a face like a praying mantis, a very thin face. Now she really *was* mannish.

There was a hill near the school, and on that hill there was a brothel, and there were also a lot of temples. Kōzuki lived near there, and Yoko Watanabe would often go round to play. It was a brownstone house. When I went past there first thing in the morning on my paper round, the two of them would throw stones at me. It felt as if they were saying "Get out of here!" She could be pretty scary, was Kōzuki-kun. Although Watanable-kun wasn't so scary.

I lost touch with Kōzuki in the second year of high school. That was when she went to Takarazuka. Yoko Watanabe came from a wealthy family, so she went to the elite girl's high school in Kumamoto. With that man's face of hers.

They both disappeared. Only I was left.

Recently I've been back to Yamaga a few times, and I've been past the bicycle shop more than once, but the shutters were always down. Not that I was that interested, since she was no beauty. She looked like a zombie. Although she did have various talents. She could run fast. Her weapon was her voice. She had an incredibly powerful voice. That voice could tear a dishcloth. So I guess she *was* kind of scary, at least in that department.

The Fourth Conversation

March 3, 2007

The weather was cloudy but warm, and there was a touch of spring in the air. As Kimitsu and I walked to the Apollo coffee shop, a friend of his came down the street on his bicycle and genially greeted Kimitsu with "hey look, it's Hitler!" This seems to be a nickname of Kimitsu's. "It's because I draw all those pictures (of Nazi soldiers, etc.)," he explained.

Settled down in the Apollo, I asked Kimitsu to tell me more about his school days. He soon got back to the topic of girls.

I went to mixed schools for junior high and senior high. I'd fancy a girl now and then but I never had a fixation. It's the same now. I may think "that woman's got a nice smile on her today, that old lady's still kind of pretty even now she's eighty"—but I'd never actually speak to a woman. Relations between men and women—well, they all end up with fighting don't they. It's the same in England I expect? It's important to keep a certain distance, I would say.

I was in love with Kōzuki, though. I'd never seen such beautiful features. They didn't have photos of pretty women in the magazines those days. They'd have pictures of Mussolini. Women to me were something like the Venus of Milo. Gods. Things one mustn't approach.

In those days we school kids didn't have the tradition of going on "dates." It was later, after I joined the Self-Defense Forces, that I first had anything to do with women. When I was a high-school boy I'd see a couple out on a date, and I'd think, "lucky old them, they've been and gone and done it." I was also very jealous of the American soldiers. Always playing around with women. And getting away with it if they caused any trouble.

You know they found those fossilized skeletons in northern Italy. They seemed to be the skeletons of a young man and woman who'd been killed while locked in an embrace. I saw it in the Sunday Mainichi. An Italian archaeologist dug them up.[40] They'd been having sex under age, so they were stoned to death. Because they threatened the social order. They were from different tribes so their love was forbidden, something like that. I think that says it all. You can't violate the laws of God, or the orders of your parents. In the end, it's all wrong when the authority of the father is too strong.

However, in my own case my parents didn't have that much authority over me, and I was brought up in relative freedom. I was always drawing pictures. Especially military pictures. American soldiers—they were my ideal of manhood. They gave me bubblegum, too. They looked like the ancient Greek and Roman soldiers that I'd seen in picture books. They had blue eyes and blond hair.

What, all of them?

Well of course there were some dark-haired ones too, and even some black men.

I think Yoko Watanabe might have been happier if she'd been born a man. Nowadays you hear a lot about Gender Identity Disorder. A problem of genetic balance. She had a woman's hair, but the face of a Neanderthal. Her teeth stuck out all over the place. The truth is that a human being is a perfect thing, but every man and woman is missing a part of that perfection.

The teachers often spoke about the war. One of them had been wounded. He'd lost a little finger. He often told us boring war stories. "Here we go again," I'd think to myself. "We lost, but he still makes such a big deal of it." I can sort of understand what we went to war for, but some of the things we got up to . . . kidnapping Koreans to pressgang them into the war effort and so on . . . were all wrong.

I had no dream for the future. It was all I could do to stay alive from one day to the next. Every day, a dance of fools. No time-outs. Wandering around and bumping into stuff. Economic problems in the background. A deer about to be eaten by a lion. No leisure to think about the future. I was living like a wild animal. The life of a brute.

However, since my family was concerned about appearances, I did go to senior high school although we couldn't really afford it. After all, I was the oldest son of a former banker. If someone was born into the kind of poverty I experienced and had a navvy for a dad and a bar girl for a mum, they'd probably end up being a yakuza or a criminal. Of course there's a genetic element to it as well. You'd end up playing on the center court at the Old Bailey. Like the hero of John Bunyan's *Pilgrim's Progress*. If you choose a bad road, then punishment surely awaits you—in America it could well be the death penalty.

I delivered the newspapers, I listened to music . . . I didn't study much. I knew my parents didn't have the money to send me to university, so I half gave up on that. "This won't work," I thought. I was in what Freud calls a state of castration. I had no power. I had no vitality. I was close to that state of castration.

I didn't feel like studying at senior high school. It was much more fun delivering newspapers, watching movies and drawing pictures. I'm sure there are many people here in Kotobuki who have suffered much more than I ever have. People with plenty of ability who never had the chance to get an education. In the end it all boils down to economics. Though many people don't want to admit it, because they don't want to lose face. They'll come up with some elegant philosophical explanation, but in the end the problem is money.

If I had the stuff that goes in an atomic bomb, I'd show off too. A man with no power can do nothing but become a philosopher. They have no weapons, so they become artists or poets. For people with no vitality, like Andy Warhol, that's the only option. Most Japanese are like that. Their bodies are small and they have no negotiating power either. That's why they make things with their hands. Cars and computers and machines. Because their bodies are small. Say what you like, but there is such a thing as national character. Indian people have incredible calculating ability. I think they'll do incredible things in the IT industry.

I graduated senior high school in Showa 34, that's 1959. The Vietnam War hadn't started yet. Eisenhower was still president. The Americans were limiting themselves to sending military advisors and commandants. The domino theory that was dreamed up by John Foster Dulles during the Eisenhower years was fundamentally wrong, but even Kennedy believed it. That was Kennedy's greatest fault.

Funny—John Lennon and I were born in 1940, Guru Nakazawa was born in 1950, and you were born in 1960, Tom-san. Makes for easy calculations, eh? A decade at a time.

When I left school I thought I'd have to earn a salary somehow, so I joined the Self-Defense Force. It was interesting. The rules were strict, but all the people who went in had lots of personality defects—just like me—so we got on well. Fellow samurai. A society of knights. Like the crusaders. It's because there are no women there that such an ideal society can be created, even if just for an instant. When women come in everything gets spoiled. I'm not talking about gays. But I do think there's a need for beauty among fellow men. However, the war was long over, and there was no particular prospect that we'd have to do any real fighting. So we felt more like boy scouts than soldiers. Or some sort of high school club. "You maintain soldiers for a hundred years to prepare for a single moment." That's how it was at the Battle of Sekigahara.[41] There's a movie on the theme too . . . the theme of how great it is to be a soldier in peacetime, just gambling and drinking all the time. One of those films starring George Peppard, I think.[42]

We did basic training at Sasebo, near Nagasaki. In a time of peace, there really is nothing more refreshing to the spirit than to become a soldier. There wasn't going to be any war. If something cropped up, the Americans would take care of us, we reckoned. So it felt like a sports club. There wasn't a particularly powerful militarism about the place. There was an American overseer, you see, and if one of the Japanese officers got violent and slapped us around, he'd be fired right away. That was very reassuring. And they even gave us money . . . about 6,000 yen a month in those days.

I learned how to use a machine gun and a bazooka. They have tremendous destructive power. It was fantastic. Great fun. I became slightly manly. Taking responsibility for my own decisions. I think the British tradition of getting the royal princes to serve in the armed forces is a good one.

Since there were no women around, life in the army was fun. We were allowed to have a few drinks, we just had to watch our language. Because the power of women is so strong.[43]

Youngsters today should go into the army. They've got no discipline, they've got no culture, they're not brought up strictly enough. I think yakuza children are better brought up as a matter of fact. Ironically enough. Because they'll get killed if they mess around.

Once we'd finished training for the day, the sergeant would take us on a tour bus to see the sights of Nagasaki and thereabouts. It really was like a boy scouts' outing. I did six months at Sasebo. Three months of basic training then three more of specialized training. In my case that meant driving a truck. That was fun too, it felt like going on a merry-go-round. It was brilliant. I got my license at the first time of asking—passed the test at the Nagasaki Board of Public Safety. It cost me a handling fee of 350 yen. If I'd not been in the army it would have cost me 100,000, maybe 200,000 yen.

The senior officers had a bit of class, but the sergeants were a rough lot. They were like the site bosses who kick the day laborers around. Like pirates, or bandits. No culture. Drunk all the time. Buying prostitutes. Kicking their subordinates. [English] *Foolish bastards.*[44] But that very kind of fault is what makes a sergeant a sergeant. If you look at fictional sergeants, like the one in Norman Mailer's *The Naked and the Dead*, or Herman Wouk's *The Caine Mutiny*, or William Bradford Huie's *The Execution of Private Slovik*, based on the Slovik incident concerning the only case of an American soldier being executed for desertion in World War II . . . what you get from all of these is that a sergeant is in a sense a class traitor. He's a working class man who will rat on fellow working men by reporting them to the gentlemen of the officer class. On the other hand, when it comes to war, the sergeant is the most reliable guy in the unit. That sort of image of the sergeant could be found in the SDF too.

Once we had completed training we moved to Hokkaido—to the Makomanai base at Sapporo. The base had previously been used by an American unit—the Oklahoma State Guard, under General Weber.[45] They had previously served about three years on the front line at the Korean War. They left in 1953. The facilities were very much in the American style. A kind of log cabin feel to it. Western-style toilets. English-language signs. It had a library, a gymnasium—all sorts of stuff. It was a totally different feeling from a Japanese-built base. The library was really big. I went there all the time, listening to records and stuff. Ordinary Japanese bases have libraries too, but they're miserable, pathetic little places, because they don't have much of a budget.

It's quite a way from Hokkaido to Kyushu. They're at opposite ends of Japan. It was very hard to go home for visits. That was before they built the Seikan tunnel, so you had to take the ferry between Hokkaido and Aomori. I wasn't used to it, and I got horribly sea sick. Ugh.

One day, when I was doing some road-building work, I had an accident. We were working like navvies on the orders of the sergeant. In the middle of some heavy rain, I was with a couple of other guys, trying to lift and carry a heavy concrete block. The conditions were so bad that we ended up dropping the block. It came down on my index finger and squashed it flat. The bone was sticking out. That was the first time I'd ever set eyes on my own bones.

Figure 3.2. Kimitsu's accident, drawn by Kimitsu.

I spent about ten days in hospital, and that finger remains painful to this day—when winter comes. The doctor did his best, and stuck the finger together again. But even so I couldn't drive anymore. Nor could I pull the trigger on a gun anymore. Though I daresay that if I'd been a carnivore like Arnold Schwarzenegger I might have been able to carry on working. If I'd been a roast beef guy or a steak guy, you know? But on rice and miso soup? I decided it would be better to quit. Japanese people have this tendency to give up rather easily.

Of course, being a driver, I shouldn't have been doing heavy labor like that in the first place, but it was an order from the sergeant. If that accident hadn't happened, I'd probably have carried on in the SDF. It wasn't just the injury itself that got to me. It was the unfair order that led to it. I felt no good would come of staying in the SDF if they were going to boss me around like that. For a commanding officer I dare say it's an amusing occupation, but for a private second class . . . I got to thinking I might end up doing myself a bigger injury.

(When I first interviewed Kimitsu in the mid-1990s, he said he had quit the SDF because he liked a drink and felt it was dangerous for a man like him to drive a truck. When I mentioned it to him, he admitted it might also have been a factor.)

Anyway, Yokohama was a pretty interesting town, and there were lots of Americans there. So I figured I'd quit the SDF and go to Yokohama. I felt I'd had enough of the SDF anyhow—let's do something different, I thought. I wanted to be like Samuel Johnson—pile up all sorts of experience and become a human encyclopedia. Because that's the more relaxing way to go—being a generalist rather than a specialist. Someone like Johnson, or maybe H. L. Menken.

Actually when I first came down to Yokohama, I worked for a spell at the Nissan Motor plant at Namamugi. I lived in a cheap apartment not much different from a flophouse, and one day the guy next door said he could get me some laboring work. So I went along with him. I started using the day labor market at Harappa in Kawasaki, later Kotobuki in Yokohama and for a few years, San'ya in Tokyo.

Wasn't it slightly odd to quit a top-flight company like Nissan to work as a casual laborer on building sites?

Not at all. In those days Nissan only paid 900 yen a day, and the navvying paid 1,500.

Those figures did not seem to match the paltry 6–7,000 yen a month that Kimitsu said was his pay in the SDF. But he insists the figures are right—SDF personnel weren't paid much in his day, he says—they were supposed to be grateful for the free food and lodging.

The Fifth Conversation

March 10, 2007

Arriving at Kimitsu's room, I heard the sound of jazz piano coming through the metal door. It was my brother Nick's CD, which I'd lent him on my previous visit. Kimitsu was sitting on his futon (which he never folded away, aired or cleaned), listening to the music and trying to draw a picture of brother Nick from the photo on the CD sleeve. It was well drawn but bore little resemblance to my brother. Like all Kimitsu's sketches of people, it looked like a blond Nazi concentration camp guard. In the picture Nick is being praised by Sir Thomas Beecham, who thinks he will be the next Peter Nero—the famous American jazz pianist who is one of Kimitsu's musical heroes. He might even make him so popular ("enthusiastic") that he might take over from the Beatles. As he practices (drilling piano working), his excitement leads to a string of expletives. "I got it! Brady (bloody) bastard bitch!"

Figure 3.3. Tom's brother Nick playing the piano.

The weather was bright and sunny, so we went for a picnic in Ōdōri Park. I had a meat dumpling, a pizza-flavored dumpling and a "Baum Küchen"

German-style cake, with a bottle of green tea. Kimitsu had a "one-cup" of saké with no food—his usual lunch. Then we headed back to the Apollo. He read the print-out of our previous conversation and spotted an error.

I noticed a mistake in the record of our last conversation. You wrote, "It was all I could do to stay alive from one day to the next. Every day a dance of fools. No time-outs." But I didn't say "dance of fools" (*ahō dansu*), I said "affordance" (*afōdansu*). It's a biological thing really. A kind of natural science that goes beyond genetics, beyond Darwin. J. J. Gibson, the American psychologist, came up with it. What he says is that people don't actually see things with their eyes or hear things with their ears—rather they are shown things, or allowed to hear things—afforded those experiences. The earth beneath our feet affords us the act of walking; a chair affords us the act of sitting. When a child gets born in the natural world, it has to be protected from lions. There are no walls in the house to afford protection. And when I was a kid, there was no affordance for me to think about the higher things; in the post-war chaos, we just had to struggle for survival every day.

It's related to the concept of autopoiesis, which is being studied in Brazil and Chile by the likes of Humberto Maturana and Francisco Varela. Shinichi Nakazawa takes those concepts seriously too.[46] Affordance and autopoiesis are the biggest discoveries in natural science since Watson and Crick discovered DNA. Professor David Bohm at London University was involved too.[47]

The matter of Armageddon is related too. Once in a thousand years you have some colossal natural disaster, and after that the human race has to start again from zero. The likes of Aum Shinrikyō and David Koresh[48] made good use of this concept. I believe the terrorists of today are doing the same kind of thing. Islamic terrorists are just like that, and what they're doing actually has nothing to do with the Muslim faith.

Personally I don't believe in Armageddon. Since the death of Communism, we've not seen the birth of a particularly attractive system of thought to take its place. All that's left is new religious cults peddling their groundless beliefs to people who feel weak and tired. They have the ability to grab the minds of such people. They do market research. They're salesmen, turning the human spirit into a commodity. Pulling on people's hearts like a magnet. Religion gives you the ability to encourage yourself. But I don't go to the shrine or the temple. There's something not right about organized religion. It's got risks but no merits.

We discussed the controversial comment made in January 2007 by Hakuo Yanagisawa, Japan's Minister of Health, Labor and Welfare, that "women are machines for giving birth to children."

That's Adolf Eichmann talk. Or some line you might find in a story by Karel Čapek. Pure robotism.[49]

The conversation didn't really get going today. I was tired and accidentally nodded off in the middle of it. The mama-san of the Apollo gave me a good scolding: "This isn't a hotel, young man!"

We decided to call it a day and went for a drink.

The Sixth Conversation

March 24, 2007

Rain.

For some reason Kimitsu was in the mood to speak in English today. As usual, I have used italics when he is speaking in English.

I was a very angry young man. I was foul mouthed, I swore all the time. I was like a meteorite. I was only a private second class, but I insulted the soldiers around me, got into drunken fights. The next morning, I'd think, what on earth was I going on about last night? Oh the shame of it! *In the morning, I think it's a bloody shame. No good. It's a cycle. That's why I quit the military. Recognized I am no good. Bloody no good. Against god, against Buddha. So I ran away. Ran away. Away. I have nothing to do. Nothing great. So anyway, ran away. Went down from Hokkaido to Yokohama. So it began. Free time.* A navvy. Day laboring at a time before the era of high economic growth set in. *Almost poor people, like young boys in Ireland, London's East End. So I go into Yokohama, construction sites, port lighterman. 1970. Same work, Pūtaro (day laborer) work, until about 2001. Along the coast, warehouses, on the ship. Like England, Thames River lighterman.*

(*Why did you choose Kotobuki, rather than the bigger doya-gai in Tokyo, San'ya?*)

San'ya is inland; it's only bloody construction sites. It's baaaad, payment is no good. So Yokohama is open to ocean, foreign, money pay very good. Money is regulated by the International Longshoremen's Labor Union, based in Chicago. So its payment is regulated. But dokata (navvies), construction sites, particular people, son of the boss, you get 10,000 yen, but for ordinary guys, you get 8,000, you get 5,000. It's particular, it's quite bad. Just read Eric Hoffer, American philosopher and longshoreman.[50] *So Yokohama was attractive. Quite bloody attractive. San'ya is inland. But my favorite is water, shoreline, waterfront, Blackpool, Frisco Bay, water . . . South-*

ampton, Blackpool, Liverpool. And many ships, vessels, German, Holland, England, America vessels.

No doubt about it—longshore work is much better than building work. In construction the wages are low and there's a lot of violence.

First I found work in Kawasaki, construction sites. Then I worked for Toyo Senpaku (a shipping company), night work, unloading bananas. I can still remember the man who first introduced me to dock work. A very tall man. I was 28, and one morning I was late looking for work. I got up at 8am, but everyone else started looking for work at 6am. He was on his way back from the night shift, and he'd obviously been drinking. He called out to me, "Hey you, why don't you go and work on the bananas? Right over there." I went where he said, and there was a microbus and a street recruiter handing out papers. "Yes, you, four more needed, yes you, three more needed . . . "

Figure 3.4. The pleasures of longshore work—taking a break on a Brazilian freighter.

I love Latin music, especially the bossa nova, and I much enjoyed taking a cigarette break and listening to that music with the Brazilian ship-hands. (Mimes bossa nova dancing). I felt as if I were connected to Brazil, and I really felt like diving into the sea and swimming to Brazil. The ship hands all had these cassette players that they'd carry on their shoulders while they listened to the music. The other ships were good too, but the Brazilian ones were the best.

On the day Princess Anne married Captain Mark Phillips, I happened to be working on a British freighter that had just arrived at Yokohama's Yamashita port from Cape Town with a cargo of coffee bags. I went up on the deck and offered the captain my congratulations. He invited me to join him for a glass of wine during the lunch break. Those were the days.

The Seventh Conversation

April 15, 2007

I arrived at Kimitsu's room around 1pm, but it was three days after Kimitsu's birthday and the weather was too good to waste in the dark interior of the Apollo café, so instead we went to Yamashita Park for a picnic. Facing out to sea next to the dockyards, this is one of the most popular hang-outs in Yokohama. I had red wine and cheese crackers; Kimitsu just drank shōchū. We sat in front of the Hikawa-maru—a beautiful old steam ship permanently moored off Yamashita Park—and made rude comments about the passers-by. Then we went to BankART Studio, a trendy art gallery in a large disused warehouse. There was an exhibition on the theme of makeshift dwellings for use in case of a major earthquake, and we enjoyed sitting in the little shacks made of newspapers, plastic bottles, supermarket bags, etc. We carried on drinking. It was very pleasant.

Figure 3.5. At the BankART studio earthquake exhibition.

Kimitsu told me that he had recently used his welfare money to make another trip back to Kyushu. But his back was hurting so badly that he only got as far as Kumamoto before turning back without reaching his hometown of Yamaga. It was a crazy story, because Kumamoto is over 95% of the way from Yokohama to Yamaga. If he was in too much pain to go to Yamaga, surely the return trip to Yokohama would have been much worse?

"No, if I couldn't get back to Yokohama I wouldn't be able to carry on living."

The Eighth Conversation

April 18, 2007

I called in at Kimitsu's room and told him I would wait for him at the Apollo. When Kimitsu arrived just after, he brought with him a stranger he had just met in the street. He was a blond American lad in his twenties with a very pale, rather unhealthy-looking face. His name was Vivian 'Vinnie' Gorman and he said he came from Utah. Like many foreign travelers, he had googled for "cheap hotel Yokohama" and ended up in one of the converted flop-houses in Kotobuki catering to backpackers. The moment he saw him, Kimitsu had warmly invited him to join us at the Apollo. Guessing from Vinnie's appearance, Kimitsu asked him if he was Jesus Christ, or possibly a Viking. Vinnie said that as a matter of fact he had heard that his father's ancestors were from Norway. Kimitsu asked what had brought him to Yokohama. It turned out he was a contestant in "Magic, the Gathering," a fantasy card game organized by a firm called "Wizards of the Coast." This game is so popular that it has a pro tour. There were 400 contestants at the Yokohama event, competing for a purse of $40,000. Neither Kimitsu nor I knew anything about it.

"He's a bird of passage," said Kimitsu. "Like one of those adventurers in Rider Haggard." His racial stereotyping got steadily worse. "Like a pirate. I'd name him 'Dark Pit' (a mysterious emptiness, with a passing reference to Brad Pitt?). 'Dark' is romantic. There's a feeling of vitality about him. A seafarer, like Francis Drake."

He introduced me in English. "Tom is Fraser![51] He's a correspondent from another dimension." Vinnie seemed quite bemused and left after 20 minutes.

That guy Vinnie has pirate blood in him. Where's that pirate walking now, I wonder? He's probably made himself disappear by magic. He's probably gone back to the sea.

I like stories about the sea. Like Graham Greene's *Brighton Rock* or Joseph Conrad's *Typhoon*. In the end, people are saved by the sea. Stories of the desert, like Steinbeck's *Grapes of Wrath*, are hard to endure. California's turning into a desert. In a way desert people are the most modern. Because they're furthest from the sea. The sea—that's what everybody yearns for. I love Turner's seascapes in oils. That dark sea, caught in an instant of a storm. We humans are water-based animals. So the sea has a calming effect on us. Rivers won't do. You still feel a little insecure with a river. Even one like the Rhine. For looks, you cannot beat the Baltic. During the Cold War, there were these prisoners who escaped from camps in East Germany or Czechoslovakia, and they got away by going underwater up the Vistula River, breathing through long straws, until they reached the Baltic. Sure enough—what they ultimately yearned for was the sea. I saw the news of those escapees on the Movietone News at the cinema. So I guess it's a fact that rivers hold out the prospect of escape.

The Movietone News made a big impact on me. For instance I remember when Charles Whitman of Texas University, afflicted by a brain tumor, went up to the top of a tower in Texas and killed about 16 people by shooting randomly into a crowd.[52] I saw that on the newsreel in the cinema. Somehow it felt even sadder because he had the same surname as the poet Walt Whitman. Then there was that case where Robert Smith barged into a beauty parlor in Phoenix, Arizona, and killed five customers, just like that.[53] But the Whitman incident had a power all of its own. They filmed it from helicopters. Then there was this alcoholic called Richard Speck, who got into a hospital and killed eight people. Most of the victims were Filipino nurses.[54] Speck was living in Chicago's Skid Row district and that was the first time I learned the word "Skid Row." It turned out Speck was virtually homeless.

Checking on the Internet later, I found that Kimitsu's recollection of these three incidents was largely accurate. They all occurred within four months of each other in 1966, and the cumulative impact of seeing them on the big screen evidently made a powerful impression on Kimitsu.

British serial murderers? Well, I am interested in Ian Brady and Myra Hindley.[55] But British society isn't as violent as America. Just look at what happened at Virginia Tech. (*Two days earlier, a Korean student had gone berserk and killed 32 students and staff there, wounding another 17.*) America is in a state of civil war. It's just as Colin Wilson says—America is not a complete culture. It's barbaric. The only thing that can control that society is English rationalism. The barbarians who dropped atom bombs on Hiroshima and Nagasaki hardly match the innocent name of the *Mayflower*. They're outlaws. Outlaws like Jessie James or John Dillinger. Americans have to develop a more Mongol approach. With all that land they've got they shouldn't be going to war with a titchy little country like Japan.

Kimitsu showed me some family photos. One of them showed his younger brother, bespectacled and balding, standing in a hotel corridor in a hotel dressing gown. A couple more showed the members at a family gathering. They were gender-segregated—one showed a group of middle-aged and elderly women, the other a group of middle-aged and elderly men. A fourth photo showed Kimitsu himself, sitting in a chair in a hotel room, looking as though he was in complete despair.

Well, about three years ago, my brother came to visit me. He stayed in a room on the top left-hand corner of the Garden Hotel. It was the first time I'd seen him in nearly thirty years—since our dad's funeral. Dad died at the age of 62. Around 1970 it was, after the Osaka expo. I reckon my dad died from the stress of living in a poor environment. His house was little more than a shack. When I saw the British movie *Saturday Night and Sunday Morning*, I noticed a very similar house there. (That movie has brilliant music, by the way—by the Hollyridge Strings.) Anyway, I was amazed to see that little shack. "So English people live in places like this!" I thought. "The workers of the world are all alike." I loved the scene where the oldest son chucks his dad's fish and chips on the floor and stomps out slamming the door behind him.

I vividly remember the day of my father's funeral.

My father worked for a public food distribution corporation under the auspices of the Ministry of Agriculture. His salary was terrible. Nearly all the top management had parachuted into their jobs after retiring from the ministry.

By the time I got home, my father had already died, and the casket was standing on its trestles. The undertakers were going about their work in the usual way, and it felt like, "when someone snuffs it, this kind of work has to be done." But when we had finished the ceremony at the graveside I spotted this young woman running away from near the grave. "Could that be dad's mistress?" I wondered. My mother was studiously ignoring her. But as for me, I said nothing but I thought "I see!" My father was an amateur photographer, and he had his own darkroom. And in that darkroom, there was a nude photograph of a woman who looked just like that woman who was running away from the grave. In the photograph she was lying down and showing her thighs, like Christine Keeler.[56] This was in the time before TV had got established, and photography sessions for nude photographs and women doing sexy poses in swimsuits were very popular. When I was a kid my father used to say "I'm going to Amakusa to take photos," and then he'd disappear for a while. Lust—that's one thing that hasn't changed over the ages. It can't be helped. It's a way to deal with stress. I don't see anything wrong with it. He paid for it properly, too. It's the beauty business. When I was a kid I used to help out in the darkroom sometimes, and I saw some incredible things then. If I'd spilled the beans there'd have been quite a rumpus—but I never did. Am I to blame for that?

I went home from Yokohama on the bullet train. The funeral was held at Yamaga. The service at the crematorium was for close family and friends only, but there were a few more people there for the funeral itself. We ordinary folk don't understand the process of a funeral, so we just do as we're told. It costs money, too. When someone important dies, like his majesty the emperor, or King George VI (now there was a manly king!), then the order of ceremonies is decided by tradition and known by all. But if it's just an ordinary person, you just get told "hey you, do that!"

There were quite a few people there, from my dad's company and so on, but I wasn't interested. I was thinking how I wanted to get back to Yokohama as soon as I could and have a drink. I was sad about my father, but I didn't see the need for such an extravagant funeral. My sister and brothers hadn't changed. If anything I reckoned I was the one who'd changed. We got on very well. We had fought when we were children, but everyone gets on with their siblings once they've passed twenty. I told them honestly that I was working as a docker. Well, it wouldn't have done to tell folks I was a professor at Tokyo University, eh? Though there are some people who tell lies when they go back to their hometown.

Twelve years before, Kimitsu had described his father's funeral in much bleaker terms, saying (in English) "My brothers and cousins beat on me. Say 'bastard! Go back to Yokohama.' Only my mum defend me."

After that, I hadn't met my brother for about thirty years, and there had been no letters or phone calls. Strange to say, if you've got a pair of brothers, each of them kind of knows what the other is doing, even if they don't see each other. It's not telepathy exactly, but you don't really feel the need to go out of your way to write letters and things.

I dragged Kimitsu back to the topic of the photographs and his younger brother.

There were four of us kids. I was the oldest son and he was the last-born. We have an older sister above us, and a brother in between us. That other brother had been driving between Osaka and Fukuoka when a taxi crashed into him and killed him. My little brother had come to tell me about that. I guess that photo of me was taken just after I heard the news. No wonder I look messed up.

My kid brothers were gentle souls, but I often got into fights with them when we were kids. I was bigger than them, so I bullied them. I somehow got it into my head that as the oldest son I had some kind of imperial authority, and I fear I committed a number of crimes against them. Especially towards the brother who was my immediate junior. He was only a year younger than me, so there was a sense of rivalry. I was an A-class war criminal. But there was no deep meaning to it. For a start we were just kids. And I did provide some brotherly services—drawing pictures for them, making paper theatres and jack-in-the-boxes for them. But since we were a defeated nation it didn't seem to matter much how we behaved—it was all kind of empty. It was as much as we could do to keep ourselves fed.

My surviving brother is an engineer at Matsushita Electric, though he's up for retirement this year. He lives in Osaka these days. He's married with two daughters. One of them went to Kyoto Seika University. My brother has a round face, but his children have long faces, like their mother. The genes seem to have gone through the mother's side. She looks slightly Caucasian. Enviable. A face like a cucumber.

The reason we finally met up again was in connection with the insurance claim following our other brother's fatal traffic accident. He had no wife or children, so the large sum of money paid out by the insurance company went to the siblings. My brother needed my signature to consent to having the money paid to himself and our sister. That's what he'd come for. I expect he'd traced my whereabouts through the SDF. Because they'd have my serial number. Or maybe he got hold of my certificate of residence or something.

Did it not bother you that the first time your brother came to see you in thirty years was to get you to sign away your share of an insurance claim?

Not really. It can't be helped. I didn't want to profit out of my other brother's death anyway. It would be far more appropriate for me to pay out condolence money. I was the oldest son, and I failed to protect my kid brother—a shameful thing. The position of an older brother is totally different to that of a younger brother.

When my brother came to see me, he was kind enough to bring with him some photos of the ceremony to mark the third anniversary of my mother's decease. I think she passed away around 2001. He told me about our mother's death in an express letter shortly before he came to see me... three years after the event. He didn't tell me about it at the time it actually happened. Probably because everybody thought I'd already died in the gutter in Kotobuki by then.

That's my older sister on the right, in the black. Not all the others are wearing black. The lady in the middle with the glasses is my mother's younger sister, the youngest of four siblings. She has to go around in a wheelchair these days, because of her rheumatism.

In the men's photo, that's my younger brother with his back to the camera, and that bald old fellow in the middle with the glasses is the husband of my wheelchair-bound aunt. He made it to subsection chief in the Kumamoto prefectural government. He went to Australia and took part in the negotiations on beef trade between Kumamoto and Australia. During the war he was a major in the army and took part in the fall of Singapore. The other men are teachers at elementary and junior high school. They're all solid citizens. *Hard people.*

I miss my mother. She was a good person, but she made a couple of mistakes. First, she went and married a man with no economic power. And her other mistake was to get married just before the war . . . she should have given that a miss. Mind you, she did a lot better than some women. At least her husband wasn't killed in the war. If I'd been a woman of her age at the time, I wouldn't have got married. And if I'd been a man, I wouldn't have joined the army either. I'd have found some nifty way to escape.

I think Kimitsu meant "respectable," rather than "mean" when he called his relatives hard people. But the image of comfortable middle-class prosperity that the photos exuded was revealing. The gap between these images and Kimitsu's stinking doya room was vast. It also made me wonder how come Kimitsu's father, a banker and man of culture, had ended up "losing his economic power" and, by Kimitsu's account, ending his year living in a house little better than a shack. And then there was the final photograph: showing Kimitsu sitting in his brother's hotel room, looking totally devastated. I guessed the photo had been taken just after Kimitsu learned of his other brother's tragic death. But why would his younger brother photograph him in such a tragic state and then, presumably, send Kimitsu a print of the photo later?

These thoughts occurred later. For now, I asked Kimitsu to tell me more about "affordance," since I was still struggling to understand the term he brought up in the fifth conversation.

OK, let's imagine a hierarchy composed of George VI, a general, a soldier and a worker. In the old days that would have been all right, but nowadays we have a democratic society that rejects such rigid class hierarchies. If you want an analogy, consider the Cro-Magnon and Neanderthal men of the Stone Age. Theirs was a tough, pressurized existence, constantly having to protect themselves from lions, wolves and vultures. Their brains developed through a process of neural Darwinism, so that they could protect themselves better. Wild beasts would come to attack them; so too would the neighboring tribe.

Then gradually their brains became more specialized, and they got to make weapons . . . guns, and then later atomic bombs. It's something that can't be helped, but the reason why humans are capable of wonderful things but do terrible things is because they lack an inclusive way of thinking. They can make better and better weapons, but they cannot fully grasp the significance of the way they use those weapons. So surely what we really need is a brain, or a philosophy, like Samuel Johnson's—a way of thought that generalizes, that brings ideas together, that can encompass the whole picture. Johnson wrote the world's first ever dictionary, and I think that kind of encyclopedic, all-encompassing mode of thought is very important.

People like Hideki Yukawa[57] and James Watt had a highly specialized mode of thought, and we need that too, but in the modern age we should think not only about utility but also about generality. At present we overemphasize utility. We no longer have lions coming at us, and there is no need to wave a gun around; therefore we no longer need our brains to develop in the direction of specialization. An end to war. This is the trend of what people call affordance.

If I understood rightly, Kimitsu meant that the environment affords modern man a far greater wealth of opportunities than it did to his ancestors; therefore we now had the leisure to think generally rather than in a specialized/utilitarian way. Moreover, general thinking was necessary to deal with the problems and dangers of the contemporary world.

Yes, what we need is a Samuel Johnson type of generalized world view. Biologists have to take an interest in Buddhism. Research chemists must also research Christianity. Marginal knowledge is called for. Superman's knowledge is needed. Self-control is needed. But in the present era, the self-control that is called for gradually becomes inhuman. Doctor Johnson predicted that . . . though there may be no records extant to prove it. We mustn't smoke. We mustn't drink. We mustn't drive, because of the environmental damage done by exhaust fumes. Self-responsibility gets heavier. That is "inhumane self-control." We can no longer do as we please. The environment reflects human lifeways, bringing hurricanes, whirlwinds and global warming as its "counter-argument." That is the response of the natural world. Nature affords human beings the opportunity to live. People have to respond to that affordance.

The massacre at Virginia Tech is related to this. That Korean kid was still thinking as if he lived in an environment like a jungle, and he responded to it violently. He didn't understand the affordance of nature, therefore he became pathological. His mistake was like thinking he was surrounded by lions, snakes and komodo dragons. It's a hallucination. That's why affordance is an interesting concept. It really is a matter of life or death—because the concept of affordance extends all the way from individual psychology to international relations and environmental problems.

I also asked Kimitsu to tell me more about autopoiesis.

Autopoiesis? Something with no input and no output, like a bootstrap.[58] A self-reproducing system. Reproduces itself without any connection to the exterior. Humans are made of proteins. Proteins make cells, cells make proteins, in an endless repetition that continues until the day we die. In the case of George Bernard Shaw, that would be a hundred years . . . in the case of Harold Wilson, a mere seventy. Autopoiesis, like a bootstrap or tensor field,[59] continues endlessly in a Hegelian dialectic, until the cells commit suicide. It always expands upwards, having no reason to move sideways. It's pure action. Shin'ichi Nakazawa is another who pays attention to it. He pursues it all the way until he achieves enlightenment. There is no extraneous noise, no extensive quantity.[60] He carries on until at last he achieves enlightenment. Nakazawa calls it a "symplectic manifold."[61]

This idea that people rise in a straight line towards enlightenment—isn't it extremely optimistic?

It's not a particularly far-fetched idea. The axiom of heat equalization, the biggest principle of entropy, also applies here. When you're young you suddenly get heated up when you see a nice young girl, and this lad at Virginia Tech got hot too, and wound up killing a lot of people and himself. It might be better to cool down to room temperature. When you're a corpse you do cool down, of course.

I later asked Kimitsu which of the following two definitions of entropy from the big Kenkyusha dictionary best matched what he had in mind.

1. In physics, one of the material values showing the thermodynamic state of a substance; expresses the degree of disorder.
2. Gradual standardization, convergence on a shared equal value; decline of quality, disintegration.

For me, it's got to be convergence on a shared equal value. Nazi Germany is the best example. They aimed at convergence, in a society where everyone was Arian.

The Ninth Conversation

April 25, 2007

Arriving at the Apollo Café and setting eyes on the middle-aged waitress.

Korean women are attractive, you know, they've got that dynamic feeling to them, half like a man. (*To the waitress*) Bonjour! (*To me*) But the women here in the Apollo are more like the motherly type. If only there were some young Korean women around here, there'd be some stimulation, and I'd be able to think of more stuff. Lust does stimulate the brain, you know.

I asked him to tell me about Kotobuki in the old days.

Nearly everyone in Kotobuki is anti-establishment. Not quite as much as the people in Kamagasaki though. People from Kansai have a certain special dynamism. I first came here in Shōwa 39; that would be 1964. It was a place made for poor folk like me. First and foremost, there was work to be had. Dock work, construction, truck driving. I'd be able to make a living. My survival pack was here.

The town was lively, like boiling vapor, like a typhoon, like a hurricane. I ate Korean-style roasted meat, I drank shōchū. I went drinking with foreigners in Chinatown. American marines, sailors from France, Germany, Britain, Indonesia, the Philippines. I had my regular bar. I learned English, but I was mostly drunk at the time, so I didn't learn anything proper. Only "panglish"—the kind of pidgin English that used to be spoken by pan-pan girls, prostitutes who hung out with foreign soldiers and sailors. No grammar. Long ago I used to see American soldiers with Japanese girls that seemed to be hanging off their powerful arms. It seemed that way because the man was so big and the woman was so small. Well, we Japanese aren't carnivores, so it can't be helped.

I had no political awareness. Left or right, it was just a matter of struggling to avoid falling by the wayside. In the old days many Japanese people died that way. In English do you have a word meaning *yukidaore* (one who has fallen by the wayside)? In England, you've always had vagabonds, but they've had some kind of skill . . . conjuring, playing the violin, juggling like that Péter Frankl.[62] True, in Japan too we've had people with trained monkeys, and the occasional woman who'll swallow snakes at a travelling freak show, but there are a lot more people who have no particular talent or skill, and they just end up dying by the wayside.

Most of the people in the far-left radical sects were from a privileged background and had been to university. But we workers were confronting lions, just living from day to day on nature's affordance. And we were lazy and played around whenever we could. We should be evolving forward, in truth, but the fact is that Japanese these days are retrogressing.

Why's that?

Because we don't have anything like those public schools you have in England. The rules aren't decided, and we're being spoiled. Everyone should do a year or two in the SDF. In Japan there's no such thing as noblesse obligé. People at the top don't take responsibility.

I objected. Surely contemporary Japan was a much more peaceful place than in Kimitsu's youth, and most people would say that society was progressing rather than regressing?

The adults are progressing but the youths are regressing. And the politicians are rubbish—because they have no policy. Still, if Japan doesn't do as America tells her we could get into trouble, so taking good care of relations with the US is Japan's survival kit. It's our raft.

In those days, the flophouses were all made of wood. There were fights all the time. Some guy would give the wall in the doya a big kick and disturb you. You'd say "Stupid bastard! Shut the fuck up!" But when you saw the guy's face it would be "Oh, you is it? Weren't we working together the other day?" So it's actually more dangerous these days. People don't have any work, so they're more desperate.

Since I'm 67, the people I know are dying like flies. Hayashi-kun's died. I'm depressed today. When you pass 60 you start losing your power. Hayashi-kun was a mild kind of guy, very quiet. We often worked at the docks together. But one day he caught cold and he took this injection for it. But it turned out the injection was contaminated with the HIV virus, and a month later he started screaming out in pain, GYAAAAAAAA! He was thrashing around on his bed, and that was the death of Hayashi-kun.

The symptoms don't sound much like AIDS . . .

This happened three or four years ago. I don't know where he came from, but he'd also been in the SDF, and he was a tough guy. A muscle man. He was 66, and I was 64 at the time. Now George Harrison has died, and he was only 58. That was a shock. He was my favorite Beatle. Too young. Like when Harold Wilson suddenly resigned the premiership when he was only 60 years old.

Figure 3.6. Clement Attlee in his youth.

I was good at fighting. Let's say I'm playing my guitar in my room, and the guy next door suddenly comes bursting in and calling me a bastard—well, there's going to be a fight. It starts with verbal abuse of course. Then throwing punches. But you know—I never lost those fights. I learned that on my arrival in skid row—that I was actually good at fist-fighting. I never started it. It was self-defense.

If it's between individuals you can make it up afterwards, but if you get mixed up with a gang of yakuza then things get a little more awkward. The Inagawa-kai is the main gang around here. I don't really want to say anything against them, because I got a lot of longshoring jobs thanks to them. It's a man's world, so it can't be helped, no? Nowadays another gang called the Sōaikai are running things in Kotobuki, with a Korean boss, but I reckon the Inagawa-kai are behind them. I think the yakuza are doing the best they can.

There was a drinking spot near where I was working, so I used to get drunk on the job. By the time I got back to my room I'd be totally oblivious . . . unconscious. The next morning I'd be woken up by one of my mates. "Wake up!" It was like being in the army. Like I was in some kind of feedback loop that had taken me back to the SDF. Sometimes I'd have regrets . . .

If I could be a college student . . . but I am not angry, just I am working to get money, and I don't care . . . still continue, like now . . . I not angry, you know. I feel no ressentiment.[63] *Just quite drunk. Night work, about 20,000 yen. But almost night shift it start from 7p.m. and end at 2 or 3 a.m. Unloading corn from ships with a shovel. If I get caught by foreman, what you do?! Bloody . . . fucking . . .*

(We got onto the topic of Japan's declining birthrate.)

I think a lot of it comes from our becoming a colony of the USA. Japanese people are short of patience and they've stopped loving each other. I think that's at the bottom of it. It's getting difficult to find house space for your dad, or your granddad or grandma. I think it might help if we had just a little more room to spare in our daily lives. It's so important to relax. Like English people do. That sense of "whatever . . . I don't care."

Turns out that the guy who killed Lucy Blackman was Korean.[64] Same as the Virginia Tech killer. It all comes from Koreans eating dog-meat instead of beef.

Ignoring Kimitsu's blatant racism, I mentioned I might get to translate Keizō Hino's novel, Yumenoshima *(1985). The title, literally meaning "Dream Island," is taken from the name of a man-made island used as a gigantic garbage dump by the city of Tokyo.*

I often worked at Yumenoshima when I was living in San'ya. Man it stank! It was weeding work. That was really tough work. The stench was unbearable. I also had a horrible boss. "Work!" "If you don't work, you don't eat!" That was no job for humans. You couldn't do it if you were hung over—you'd throw up. It was raw garbage from Ginza and Roppongi. Paid about 6,000 yen. I went five or six times. We'd return to San'ya after an hour or two. You got to do it a couple of times a month on a rotation system.[65]

Why did you go and live in San'ya?

I somehow felt like going there. I guess it was the later 1980s? I came back to Yokohama after three years, though, because the jobs ran out at San'ya. The wages for navvying were lower than at Kotobuki too. About 8,000 yen a day, and there was no dock work to be had. Dock work pays about 15,000 yen a day at Kotobuki. So I concluded that Kotobuki was better. You don't want to work like a mug. I finally realized that there was no advantage to being in San'ya. It was a rougher place than Kotobuki. The people at San'ya are a bunch of savages. It's slap in the middle of Tokyo, but they're like aborigines. They spit all over the place and they piss in the street. They're foul-mouthed and I had an extremely bad feeling about them. It's a feudal society, is San'ya, and I got to hate the whole place.

Well, various things have happened to me, but in the end it's been a happy life, so I guess it's all good. I've got a nice relaxed feeling now.

The Tenth Conversation

April 28, 2007

Well if you hadn't shown up, I'd have just carried on sleeping. I dreamed I was watching an old movie, *My Fair Lady*. "Won't you take me to the church on time."

I asked Kimitsu if he sometimes wished he had made it to the church at some time in his life.

Marriage for me was not so much a dream as a trap to be avoided at all costs. It causes all sorts of problems, like domestic violence. Better for it to remain a dream. Dreams are much more accurate than reality, and they soon end and cause no trouble afterwards.

I have a lot of dreams. Dreams of being in foreign countries. Being in a bunkhouse, and the guy in the next bed is yawning and saying stuff in a foreign language. I once dreamed I was in Coventry, U.K.

Last night I stayed up late watching an all-night politics talk show. Then it was the American baseball—Matsuzaka against Matsui.[66] Matsuzaka's a lucky so-and-so. He gets hit all over the park, but his mates score tons of runs and he winds up being the winning pitcher again. Is that fate, I wonder, or is it just luck?

I gave Kimitsu a copy of paper on homelessness by sociologist Akihiko Nishizawa. It was called Bōrei no Koe, *or The Voices of Ghosts.*

Some ghosts are very nice you know—like the ghost of Hamlet's father. In the case of Japan, since ours is a matrilineal society, most of the ghosts one sees are women, especially one's mother. It's the same in Germany. But in patrilineal countries like America or England, children are mostly brought up by their fathers . . . that was revealed in an international comparative research study that the American Defense Department commissioned just before World War II. They hired a lot of famous anthropologists—including Ruth Benedict, of course—and when the American military high command saw the results of the survey they were overjoyed. "Great!" they said, "Looks like we can defeat Germany and Japan in warfare."

Countries with matrilineal societies are weak. Men rely on women, so they are weak spirited. It's because they know they can't defeat women that they get violent towards them. And they become known for their cruelty, cunning and cowardice. Patrilineal societies are more mature. That's why great leaders emerge, like Winston Churchill or Margaret Thatcher (she's a man in my book). General Montgomery, putting up an umbrella on top of his tank—he was a loved and likeable general.

Convoys of toy-boys . . . tough women have enough power to serve in a frontline unit on a battleship.

I have no prejudice against women. There have been so many great women. Eva Peron, Barbara Castle, Simone de Beauvoir, Marie Curie, Shirley Chisholm, Gloria Arroyo, Indira Ghandi, Aung Su Chi, Madame Blavatsky. Well, Madame Blavatsky was a pretty strange person, but I don't dislike her. History always throws up maniacs like her.

Since the topic of the occult had come up, I asked Kimitsu to tell me more about his admiration for Colin Wilson.

The Outsider was a bestseller in Japan. The "Angry Young Men" were famous here as well. Wilson was living in a tent on Hampstead Heath. He had a girlfriend and he was playing around like crazy. He wrote it all down in a sex diary and just about managed to escape when he was on the point of having the shit beaten out of him by her father. Well—he was an existentialist so that was just the sort of lifestyle you'd expect him to have. But impressively enough, his writing style is always cool and shows firm self-control.

When I was at senior high school, I read a review of that book. Much later, after I had quit the SDF, I got drunk one day and wandered into a second-hand bookshop in Kawasaki. Bam! There it was. *The Outsider*. I bought it for a couple of hundred yen—which was a lot of money in those days. I read it in an all-night sitting, and it threw me into a state of excitement. Colin Wilson is my Shōkō Asahara[67] —my guru. It's no good reading a book like that when you're sober. Got to read it drunk. It's the same with De Quincey.

Wilson is always searching for what he calls "the peak experience," but I'm a bit concerned about what happens after that. After the high, there may be a comedown waiting. There's a similar problem in Buddhism. After you've achieved enlightenment, what do you do next? Still . . . I guess you couldn't lead a really depraved life after achieving the peak experience.

In the book Wilson discusses a number of culture heroes. Vincent Van Gogh, for instance. In the space of a single year, he painted *Starry Night*, an incredibly beautiful masterpiece that overflows with the pleasure of life, and found life so unbearable that he killed himself. The former of these two actions was a graphic peak experience; the latter was in a sense a similar graphic production. Van Gogh was an existentialist thinker, don't you think? Like the Dalai Lama.

I myself have never had a peak experience. I'm still looking. Maybe I have to go to Tibet for three years, like Shin'ichi Nakazawa. I bet Colin Wilson's wishing he'd gone to Tibet too. He just wasn't able to go because he came from a poor family.

What Colin Wilson has to say isn't only relevant to new religions, drugs, love etc. It's because of his universal relevance that his book was a bestseller all over the world. He sat himself down in the reading room of the British Museum and read and read until at last he found a special experience of his own amid the universal. "Search for the extraordinary in ordinary everyday life"—that is his message. In that respect he follows in the footsteps of Blake and Eliot. He hadn't been to university, he was just a vagabond playing around with women, and yet he skillfully expressed that truth. If anyone like that were to appear in Japan, he'd be killed right away.

I mentioned that I'd noticed that all the mass murders he was talking about the other day happened in the same year—1966.

Yep, 1966. And it felt like they all happened in very rapid succession. I watched TV pretty much all the time that year, and it seemed like there were an awful lot of violent American dramas. *Gun Smoke . . . Untouchables . . .* all tales of outlaws. It wasn't interactive—all you could do was sit there and watch. I think we were being brain-washed, like in Orwell's *1984*. Brain-washed with American violence.

The Eleventh Conversation

May 12, 2007

I gave Kimitsu one of my own papers, about the NIMBY issue in Japan. I briefly summarized it, and he questioned my criticism of the city of Yokohama's policy of concentrating people seen as socially problematic in Kotobuki.

It's a damn good thing there's a place like Kotobuki. This isn't some kind of apartheid you know. There's no compulsion, and the people who live in Kotobuki understand each other.

This from a man who once called Kotobuki "a prison camp" . . . the years had mellowed him perhaps.

Kotobuki's golden age, which was also the age when I was able to get regular employment as a day laborer, lasted until 1989. When the Shōwa emperor died, Korean workers flooded into Japan. Because the emperor was something like Hitler to them. You can see Japanese TV on Cheju Island,[68] so they knew he'd died. Until the emperor passed away, I often got jobs that took me to Tokyo or Ibaraki, but all that work was taken by Koreans. They eat dogs and cats, you know, so they smell dreadful.

I was dismayed to hear this from a man I had known for his tolerance and internationalism, but dutifully wrote it down anyway. He changed the subject.

I did time in prison you know. It happened when I was 42, my *yakudoshi*,[69] a sort of male menopause. For assault.

It was an act of revenge. While I was sleeping in a park, some guy came and ripped me off. He took about 30,000 yen that I had on me, along with the truck driver's license I got in the SDF. Quite some time passed after that. Then one day, about a month later—it was June—the rainy season. Very hot and sticky. I didn't think there'd be much work available that day, so I went to the Daimaru Store in the morning and started drinking shōchū there. I'd been sleeping outdoors. I saw this Indian guy getting beaten up. Then there were some yakuza fighting in the street. That was an unlucky omen. There was something ominous about the oppressive weather, too. In Buddhism there's something inauspicious about rain. So the rainy season is an unlucky time of year. They say that if you do something bad it causes rainstorms. If you have too much sex it can bring typhoons.

Anyway, along came this Indian guy who was working on a freighter. He'd been beaten up and he seemed to be in a really bad way, so I let him have some of my shōchū and tomatoes. He was extremely grateful. Just then I caught sight of the guy who ripped me off. I instantly flew into an instinctive rage. I slashed him several times in the face and chest with a knife. If I'd had a rifle I would have shot him. I'd been in the SDF, so I knew how to use one. He was damn lucky that Japan has such strict gun control laws.

I was given 30 months, but the trial took six months, during which I was held in a detention center, so I served two years after that. It was a good opportunity to do some fieldwork on the Japanese penal system. First I was in the Tokyo Detention Center, and then they sent me to Mie prison. The Ministry of Justice sends people all over the place. I did a lot of reading in prison. That's where I read *Pilgrim's Progress*.

It was frightening in prison. I never knew when I might get killed. Reading Bunyan just made it scarier still—because the book and my own environment were the same. There's a prison in Pilgrim's Progress, as you know. As Viktor Frankl[70] put it, "I had a frightening dream, but when I opened my eyes it was more frightening." I had that experience two or three times. There were yakuza in the prison, but they weren't as scary as the wardens. The wardens would give you quite a thrashing if you broke the rules. It was total war.

But I don't resent the two-and-a-half years I spent in prison. The guy I stabbed nearly died, so it was a fair cop. After I went into prison I learned that the guy I assaulted never showed his face in the workplace again. It may seem strange to speak of prison like a sort of holiday camp, but as a matter of fact prison was pretty interesting. It's harder to get into prison than to pass the Tokyo University entrance examination, you know. Only about 30,000 people manage it.[71] Apart from the ban on drinking and smoking, it was much like the SDF. Collective living. At first I didn't know how to behave. I hadn't realized that it would be almost the same as training in the SDF. They made us wear light-blue overalls with no pockets or buttons. Actually it was easier than the SDF. There were seven of us in the cell, and one thing was that you had to greet your seniors respectfully. Greeting someone for the first time meant telling them how long you were in for and what your offence was. One of them had killed his wife, but he got a reduced sentence because they'd found him to be not of sound mind at the time. Another guy was an *atariya*—someone who deliberately gets hit by cars to claim compensation money. Another was doing eight years for burning down his own house to get the insurance money. Another was a yakuza. He'd been flying to the Philippines and Taiwan to deal in amphetamines. It was pretty interesting. Guys like Oscar Wilde grew in stature while they were in prison. You can become a shaman. (In South America shamans cover themselves with poison to get the antidotes for diseases, you know.) In prison, you can see things from the standpoint of the outsider. You can see the workings of society,

My job in prison was making anoraks. We used cutters made in America to cut up the cloth to match the paper pattern sheets. Then we'd put the pieces together with a sewing machine and iron them. It was light labor—I whistled while I worked. It was full-time work from first thing in the morning, but we did have a lunch break, and physical exercise from 3 o'clock. Apart from the fact that you only got about 50 yen a day for wages, it was easier than working life on the outside. The atmosphere in the prison was good. We all knew that if we did something bad our sentence would be extended, so we behaved ourselves. The trusty prisoners that the wardens used as assistants to control the others were hardened criminals with serious or multiple offences. They'd be in for armed robbery, or they'd be doing their fourth stretch. The wardens would use them as bosses to make their own lives easier.

A prison is supposed to be a place where you think, "Abandon hope, all ye who enter here," like Dante's Inferno. But in Japanese prisons even the yakuza are well-behaved—they make it too easy. There's no corrective function at all.

I asked Kimitsu if he was really sure the man he attacked was the one who stole his money.

I don't know for sure. After all, I was asleep at the time. But he took my driving license as well, and I was really burning with anger towards the whole world. Eichmann! The case went from the district court to the high court. I tried to look for defects in the Japanese penal system. It's true I used a knife against him, but the other guy was a really nasty piece of work. A big guy, he was, and he hung out with a den of thieves. What I did was like a strategic bombing raid. There was a strong possibility he was the culprit. About a month had passed since I'd been ripped off, and I'd thought about it very carefully. If I didn't get him back, I'd be no different from a Jew murdered by a Nazi.

I appealed the first verdict, but in the end I admitted the offence. The prosecutor had nothing to do with the incident, so I couldn't expect him to understand. Not after he'd spent his cozy life in the safety zone after graduating from Tokyo University. So in the end there was nothing for it but to take the rap. If I appealed it any further I'd end up in the detention center forever, and I wanted to get back to work, so I thought "oh, whatever."

I felt sorry for Bunyan's hero. I only had six months to go when I read that book, but the guy in *Pilgrim's Progress* got ten years for armed robbery and murder.

I made a lot of friends in prison. I had a bit of status because I could draw pornographic pictures. Pictures of men and women tangled up together. There are no magazines or videos in prison, you see. I'd always have an eraser with me when I drew pictures of cunts, because I knew I'd be tortured if they found me with them on me. I used to get various requests. A music-lover would want a picture of some guitarist . . . a right-winger would want a picture of Hitler . . . a woman's butt . . . I became quite respected. Art is an aid to status.

Somehow we had drifted onto the topic of sex.

When I was in the SDF, I sometimes went with my mates to the brothels in Susukino, the entertainment district in Sapporo, but I didn't enjoy it. Being shy, I couldn't do it sober. So I'd get drunk before I went out to do it, but the alcohol would impair function. If you go with a woman at Susukino, you don't need a condom. But they say "just wait a moment," go to the toilet, and put in this round plastic thing, I think it's called a pessary. If your prick touches it, it hurts like hell. It's like a plastic veil, or a curtain, separating man and woman (see figure 3.7). I was never satisfied. And on top of that I had to pay a thousand yen. In those days a soldier's wages were around six or seven thousand yen. So I quit going with women. And with bitter memories.

Kimitsu drew a sketch on the memo pad illustrating his painful experience with the prostitutes in Susukino (figure 3.7). He also wrote various unrelated notes on the paper. The bold Japanese writing says "Pilgrim's Progress, John Bunyan (in English), Mie Prison two years six months." The fainter Japanese writing says "revitalizing the diencephalon and brain stem." The diencephalon is a part of the brain connecting the brain stem to the two hemispheres. The key to revitalizing the brain lies in the esoteric "aah" symbol on the far left of the page, which Kimitsu associates with special breathing techniques. The English words "wish," "will" and "shall" are part of a discussion on human volition and fate.

I have never slept with a woman without paying money. I have nothing to do with women. Unless I get drunk I am incapable of communication with women. And if I do get drunk and end up going up into the room, I can't do it. When all is said and done, Japan is a matrilineal society and men cannot get the better of women. And the two sexes can never fully understand each other. *Incomplete communication.*

I was a heavy reader in those days. I read Steinbeck, De Quincey, Herman Melville, Herman Hesse, Karel Čapek. So I knew it was no good blaming women for my own unhappiness, but I couldn't help feeling that what they were doing was somehow revenge for Jack the Ripper.

The reason why there are no prostitutes in Kotobuki these days is strictly economic. No one's got any money. In the days when there was plenty of longshore work, they were here all right. It's a simple matter of supply and demand.

Women have acquired the power of Amazons. Women are mature at the unconscious level. They are the mature side.

When I was in elementary school and I got a look at my father's dark room, I was embarrassed. At the time I had my big crush on Noboru Kōzuki, but still I was only an elementary school kid . . . I regret it. Afterwards I never fell in love with a woman again. I might occasionally think, "wow, she's got a big butt," but that was as far as it went.

Figure 3.7. The plastic veil, or curtain, between man and woman.

A young postman came into the café to deliver a letter.

Oh I say! *Please Mister Postman*! What a fine figure of a man! It's the first time in a while that I've seen a young man doing a solid job of work.

Still . . . it is thrilling to touch a woman. Like Dante longed to do with Beatrice. That tension. But I could never be together with a woman for long. Like with Romeo and Juliette. What a fantastic couple they made. Suffering, transformed into pleasure. But god those pessaries hurt. Agony! And you could hear this plastic sound, *paka-paka*. *It's not fun*. It was woman's revenge, that plastic gizmo. I beat a hasty retreat. *Not complete communication*. It was only a tiny little material object, but that alone was enough to turn a man into a murderer.

I was a pretty bad soldier, but looking back on it I have no regrets. There were some tough times, but I got my driving license and learned how to use a rifle, and I made some friends. And the best thing about it was that it was an all-male world. Like a temple. There was no need to have anything to do with women.

My son, then at high school in England, was shortly to sit his A Level Philosophy exam. I asked Kimitsu if he had any tips on the various topics. Below are Kimitsu's response to the exam topics with a few riders of my own.

Do miracles exist? Miracles definitely exist. You know the speed of light, right? Human bodies are made out of light, so when a Tibetan lama gets old he turns into light. From our perspective it looks like a miracle, but for an adept it's just a regular thing. Though you do have to practice extremely severe austerities. Your son should become a disciple of Shin'ichi Nakazawa.

Does God exist? *I believe in god . . . many gods. Lead me the right way.*

If God exists, how can we explain the existence of evil? *Lots of people are on the earth, so even in Japan bastard bōryokudan [yakuza], even America mafia bitch, even mainland China son of a bitch, so it's a movie actor bad. We are alternative: death or submission? Right or wrong? What do you select? Herman Hesse says planning no good, so no good planning.* (*Passionately raising his voice*) *Human being is bad, basically bad. Herman Hesse said it's no good making a plan.*

Is that fatalism? *Quite approaching existentialism. French poet Mallarme says it looks like dice, decides your fate. Making a baby . . . making a good joke . . . it's no good. Your fate is decided, so there's no point making an effort. Nothing place, so revolt, reverse, reback. I am the position of quite poor people, complete. NOT Rockefeller, Carnegie, bitch money Microsoft, I am side of poor people. People who work hard. I don't like big money, son of a bitch. (Gesturing a punch, laughing loudly). With poor people, painful people.*

Is euthanasia morally justifiable? If the person to die wishes it, I see nothing wrong with euthanasia. "I want to die." "I want some relaxation." I'd accept euthanasia if my body had packed in. "Kill me, and scatter my remains in Tokyo Bay." Might as well give the fish something to eat. While alive I've eaten a lot of salmon and tuna, so it'd only be reasonable for me to say "sorry about that—it's my turn to be eaten now. Fishes, excuse me! I ate a lot of you guys, so you can eat me now. Fishes, thank you!"

When Tibetan lamas die, they have their bodies abandoned on the mountainside, so that hawks and other birds can eat them. It's the same thing. When I die, I'd like to be chopped into pieces and left on Mount Fuji for the eagles and buzzards to help themselves. A buzzard's dessert. I'd even put the seasoning on for them. Put a pinch of salt on my head. (*Laughs*) That's the Buddhist way of thinking!

Is there any prospect of society improving in future? *It's overhead getting very good. American constitution. Liberty, saying mercy, it's a long time ago, Thomas Jefferson . . . freedom, equal, mercy . . .* (laughs) *American* *constitution. Jefferson declare, so we go . . . free . . . equality, equal, mercy* (Gesturing swimming forwards, big laugh). *Wonderful constitution! Thomas Jefferson! It's really quite a constitution.*

What about Japan's constitution? (Laughter) *It's not enough! More effort required. Japan should make more effort to pursue Thomas Jefferson, free, equal, mercy.*

Do heaven and hell exist? They both exist. Because you still have consciousness after you die. If you sleep, you see dreams, right? That's because you retain consciousness. At the moment you fall asleep, everything goes black. But after a minute or so passes, you start to see dreams. It's the same when you die. You see an intensely bright light. Then you see dreams. People who've done good things see blue dreams, like a blue moon. People who've done bad things see indescribably terrible dreams.

When I go to sleep, everything is totally black for a while, but after that I see dreams. Pretty dreams, dirty dreams. While we're alive we are constrained by our bodies, but when we die we have no such constraints, so who knows what dreams we may see. A. P. Elkin, who did fieldwork with Australian aborigines, said that among the Barthagen and Ildawongga[72] they have a myth where a man spills the blood of his pregnant sister, and a dragon comes surging up, meaning that if you defile nature, divine punishment awaits. The Ainu have similar myths. In Japan you can find that kind of myth on mount Koya or in Nagano. And Japanese do carry protective amulets of course.

Personally I don't carry an amulet, but I do recite mantras. I used to know a lot of mantras, but now I only know Shingon esoteric ones.

He closes his eyes and starts reciting a lengthy mantra.

Tibetan esoteric Buddhism. Hey—anyone would want to go to heaven when they die, right?

He closes his eyes once more and continues reciting the mantra.

When white light is refracted, *aum* is white, *bajira* is yellow, *sa* is red, and *to* is green. *Toba* is blue. The last is blue. Light with speed is blue. It's not just me saying that. I got it from Shin'ichi Nakazawa. This is the world, the essence that creates human beings. The treasure is in our forehead.

The Twelfth Conversation

May 26, 2007

Kimitsu had got me interested in Eric Hoffer and I had started reading his work, so I asked him to tell me more about him.

The first time I came across Eric Hoffer I guess I was in my thirties. It was at the time of the gas panic (the 1974 oil shock). I was living in Kawasaki at the time. It was very hard to get any work, so I would often go to the library and kill time reading. I had got to like libraries when I was in my high teens. I got into a fight with my brothers and briefly left home. I spent about three days living homeless. I spent quite a lot of that time in the library, reading Walter Scott's *Ivanhoe*. So when I found myself with time on my hands in the 1970s, I naturally went back to the library. Whenever I've been in trouble, libraries have been a sort of sanctuary for me. Long ago, Buddhist temples used to do a lot of volunteer work, but they've become so corrupt recently—the monks do nothing but eat, drink and play around. So in my case the library took the place of the temple as a place of sanctuary. When I didn't have work, I'd go to the library and read Swedenborg, Barthes, Merleau-Ponty, G. K. Chesterton, Colin Wilson, Samuel Hayakawa, Lewis Mumford, Arthur Koestler. I also read Montaigne and De Tocqueville, but they were not of the slightest use.

Getting into the habit of reading books was one positive outcome of the oil shock for me. If that hadn't happened, I'd probably have got into a dull routine of working, earning, drinking and playing, and I'd have ended up in prison just like that. Just out of negligence. But as Hoffer says, "to think deeply about things, you need to be idle." Libraries are free, so they're ideal places for when you're broke.

So I got to read Hoffer. Just picked up a book of his by chance. Hoffer? What's this? Some German guy?" Then I started reading and thought: he and I, we're molecules of the same substance . . . we're buddies . . . I can do the kind of things you're writing about!" Because I was a manual laborer, the same as him. He knew the importance of looking after your mates. He was pragmatic, so when he couldn't get work, he became a backpacker and set out for the road. That's the American spirit for you, eh? There are a lot of migrants among American longshore workers. As you can see in that great Marlon Brando movie, *On the Waterfront*.

Hoffer had a disability. He went temporarily blind when he was a child, and although his vision recovered after that, he never knew when he might go blind again. His own body was a kind of time bomb. Though being a real man, he never told anyone about it. When he became unemployed, he made the effort to go home on his own two legs. He had no education, but he started writing books, had them accepted by publishers, and wound up being a professor at the University of California. It was because he'd suffered so much that he was able to do all that. His writing is random and spontaneous. They're not academic works or novels, more like diaries. It feels like he's always ad-libbing.

During the fifties he was homeless in the Mojave Desert for a spell. He was surrounded by danger—mosquitoes, centipedes, sidewinders, scorpions, coyotes, all sorts. So he was writing from experience when he wrote "we have to do battle with nature. It's not just pretty scenery." Yes, he was pragmatic.

But isn't that spirit of battling nature partly to blame for America's environmental problems?

Well, they've overdone it, haven't they. It's all very well to battle with centipedes and scorpions, but the ozone layer is a different dimension. Anyway, if centipedes and scorpions attack, humans have got to defend themselves. But when it comes to tearing up the land in quest of oil, that's an attack on nature by humans. Same goes for the Rothschilds digging up all those diamonds. My point is that Hoffer was speaking from personal experience. Millionaires from Texas haven't had that kind of experience. Go and live in the desert for two or three days—that's Hoffer's message to those guys. Not that it's an order. He's just saying "this is what it's like." He's speaking directly from personal experience—he has that in common with Shin'ichi Nakazawa. The peak experience that Colin Wilson talks about is the same kind of thing.

Hoffer's thought is surprisingly esoteric, similar in some ways to Tibetan esoteric Buddhism, I think. The key word is "homeless." I'd not be surprised if some of the radiation left over from the Nevada nuclear tests had got into Eric Hoffer's brain and influenced his thought while he was homeless in the desert. Stark naked and sleeping in the desert. Sleeping rough—that opens the road to enlightenment.

What about homeless people in Japan?

They're different. They're victims of the political system. They're not homeless because they want to be. When Hoffer slept rough in the desert he was practicing ascetic austerities. Come to think of it, I think there's something in one of his books about positively choosing to live in the desert. It may have been an unconscious thing, but what he was doing was very similar to the austerities practiced by Tibetan lamas. Reading his works, I often think "this person doesn't feel like an American or European—more like an Asian. He's a lama."

Japan today is in a kind of spiritual recession because people are so negligent of spiritual matters. It's worse here than in America or Europe. I want to say "wake up!" to everyone, but if I did that a policeman would come and arrest me. Japanese society is sick at present, and even if I offered a prescription, it wouldn't be accepted. As you know—*Bungei Shunjū* won't publish our book.

Bungei Shunjū is a conservatively inclined publisher, one of several that rejected the Japanese edition of this book. But, I suggested, Kimitsu's view of Japanese society as having become corrupt and spiritually impoverished compared with the old days was actually a conservative view, possibly not dissimilar to how the editors at Bungei Shunjū might feel.

That old stuff about banzai for the emperor is all wrong of course, but postwar Japan has become schizophrenic. In politics it's been the Communists and Socialists against the rightists and conservatives. In warfare we were overpowered by the Americans, forced into suicidal acts like the kamikaze attacks and still defeated. And since then, there's been an overly long moratorium. I'd been meaning to say it earlier, but we just don't have the kind of expressive power that you find in Colin Wilson. Whenever I see young people today I want to call out to them "go for it!"—but if you shout stuff like that on the street you'll get beaten up by a yakuza.

So what would be your "prescription" for Japan?

Stop watching TV for once, go and climb a high mountain, and take a good slow look around you. That's what Eric Hoffer says too. Like Moses when he received the ten commandments. *(Starts drawing figure 3.8. Jehovah/Yahweh [Yach] is giving the commandments, and 'discipline,' to Moses (Moz), who is suitably awestruck).*

I suggested that Jehovah seemed a bit like a scientist, in a white lab coat.

I'd have no problem with that interpretation. After all, God does have that rationalistic side to him. Moses is the one screaming out weird irrational things. When I was a kid I thought Moses was pretty cool, but now I reckon Jehovah's the cool one.

Is Japan really spiritually worse than other countries? At least people hardly ever kill each other over religion here.

The problem is the start line. The gap's too big. Some people start the race from way out in front, others from way behind.

Figure 3.8. Moses receiving the Ten Commandments.

Starts drawing figure 3.9. It is a simple picture of two runners about to set off from different start lines, which is clearly "unfair." The Japanese word "kakusa" (differential) is also written just above. I think "knigt" is a reference to aristocrats ('knights') having a head start in life.

But Kimitsu has also written various esoteric Buddhist terms on the picture, such as the Tibetan "shinee" meditation technique which he has made several attempts to spell. There is also a diagram of Buddhist color symbolism, with the traditional color/direction associations: red/west, green/north, white/east, yellow/south. The sound of breathing ("ah") and the characters for "Shingon" (true word, the name of a major Japanese Buddhist sect) are also written, along with a reference to the Doppler effect and Kimitsu's favorite esoteric symbol, which appears twice. These words he added to the picture during the conversation recorded below.

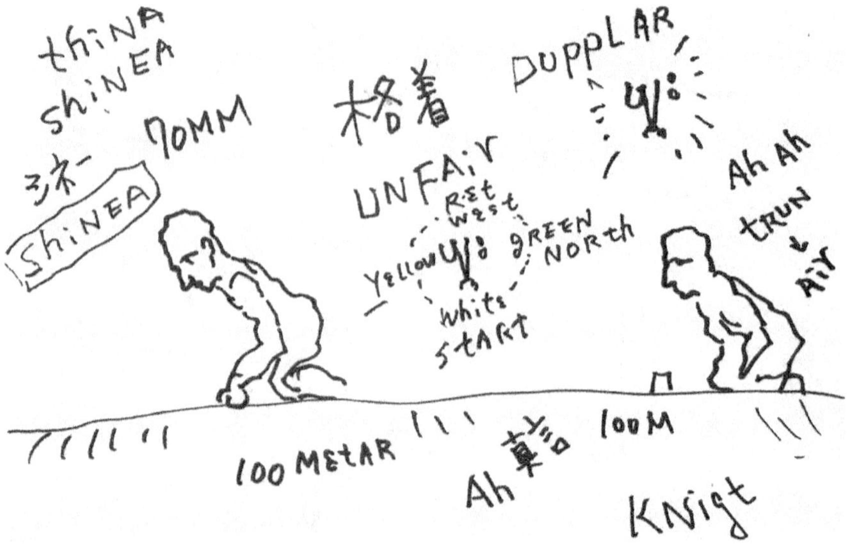

Figure 3.9. The start line.

The differentials are widening, and we're getting closer to the American model. But I have no *ressentiment*. In my own case it was my fate to become a day laborer—my karma. But Eichmann and Hitler are in hell now! They're right there in Dante's Inferno. Hideki Tōjō's right there with them too. They're all in hell! (*Laughs*). Receiving eternal punishment. It's all planned, like mathematics. People are material things, so they're always decaying, always getting closer to the end. But when you die, things can go into reverse. People who give food to stray cats and dogs when they're alive, get their reward after they've died.

What about you, Kimitsu? When you die, will you be receiving reward or punishment?

Hah! That's a tricky one. Fifty-fifty I guess. The same would go for most people, wouldn't it? I saw this British movie once, with these guys who loved fighting. They fought like a couple of moose locking antlers, over money and women and stuff. Hoffer doesn't discuss that kind of thing. He never married, you know. Same as me. The Buddha said it: Awake! Know your surroundings. That's why they do yoga. That's why they practice meditation.

I had been busily inputting. Now I looked up to see that Kimitsu had shoved a finger into his right nostril and was exhaling with the sound "aaaah." He said this was an esoteric Buddhist breathing technique, and that it somehow corresponded to an esoteric symbol which he proceeded to add to his "Start

Line" cartoon, though I don't think it had anything to do with the rest of the picture or the unequal society that it depicts. The symbol looks like the letters "u" and "v" in cursive script, with a pair of small circles resembling a colon to the right. You can see two examples of the symbol in figure 3.9: one in the middle, below the word "UNFAIR" and surrounded by the compass points and their associated colors in Tibetan Buddhism; and again, just below the word "DOPPLAR." The symbol also appears on the far left of figure 3.7, p. 73. I do not know where this symbol comes from and would be grateful if any reader could enlighten me.

Kimitsu then developed the discussion to cover Tibetan Buddhist theories linking direction, color and human physiognomy, drawing the following diagram on a serviette:

White	East	Heart/Third Eye
Yellow	South	Eye
Red	West	Throat
Green	North	Snake, sex organs

Aaaah. . . . Ah. If you breathe through your nose, it really calms you down spiritually. "Trun"—it means air. Doppler Effect, when something material slows down, it becomes heavier. Slow down and gravitational force makes you heavier, but if you speed up, you steadily approach white light. If you practice enough austerities, that is. You won't go to hell—you'll go to heaven. That's Shingon—true words.

But your face looks awfully pale Tom. You look like you're at death's door. Don't overdo things—you'd better go home. Put your finger in your right nostril. Then say "aah" and breathe through your left nostril. That'll soon bring you back to health. Esoteric breathing—can't be beat. Or even if you don't do that, concentrate on that "aah" symbol and you'll be all right.

The Thirteenth Conversation

June 2, 2007

As Kimitsu and I entered the Apollo Café, a very small, thin, weak-looking old man was just leaving. He was one of the very few regular customers at the Apollo. His hair was snow white. He walked so slowly one could barely be sure that he was actually advancing at all, with the aid of a walking stick that was covered with metal badges like that of a dedicated hill-walker. It also had various cute baubles hanging off it. When we entered the café we noticed an empty coffee cup on his usual table. Five minutes later, the automatic door slid open and the ancient man came back in. He sat at a table very near us. The Korean mama-san came over. In a very small voice, he said "I gave you a ten thousand yen note just now." "No, no sir, that was a one thousand yen note! You gave me one thousand yen, and I gave you six hundred yen change. Right?" Saying nothing in reply, the ancient rose agonizingly slowly from his seat, and, again walking so slowly one could barely be sure that he was actually advancing at all, left the café.

Distracted by the ancient, I had not been following Kimitsu's thread. He had been saying something about leprosy.

As you will know from the Steve McQueen movie *Papillon*, tropical leprosy is not a very contagious disease at all. McQueen can be seen smoking a cigarette with the lepers in that leper colony in the film. The Japanese strain of leprosy could—very rarely—be communicated by physical contact, but after the war it became totally safe. The fact that the isolation policy nonetheless continued for decades after the war[73] is down to the kind of NIMBY instinct that you discuss in your paper. Rulers can be very cruel. But at least initially, the ordinary people of Japan supported that policy too. Out of ignorance. They didn't understand medical science. It was the same with tuberculosis. Before the war a lot of Japanese died of TB in their twenties. Kenji Miyazawa went that way; so did Takuboku Ishikawa.[74] We only learned that antibiotics were effective against TB when the American forces arrived at the end of the War. It was thanks to the US military that we were able to defeat TB. I owe eternal gratitude to the American army. So do all Japanese people.

(Looking over the print-out from our previous conversation and reaching the mention of Eric Hoffer's temporary blindness.)

Maybe people need to experience blindness now and again. I rather fancy we see too much. It's probably good to shut everything out occasionally. Like in a dark room.

A fat middle-aged lady, apparently slightly mentally handicapped, entered the café. The mama-san came for her order. She kept saying "aitsui, aitsui." At last the mama-san realized that she wanted "iced tea."

Hoffer was the king of the waterfront. It's not just me who reads him. He's popular among dock-workers. (*On Hoffer's combative view of the natural environment*) It's a bit early to criticize America for environmental problems. Unlike Japan and Britain, America only has a shallow history. Because it was a colony. A country that started from an empty desert. They had to get the infrastructure sorted out first. The environment was a problem for later.

In Eric Hoffer's day, there was still a lot of need for manual labor. The docks were short-handed, and there was tons of work to be had. And it was well paid—15,000 yen a day. Young people today, those guys who sleep in internet cafés and get day laboring work on their cell phones—they're making about 8,000 yen a day. 8,000 yen! Things have greatly changed. The kind of lifestyle that I and Eric Hoffer experienced is probably impossible these days.

I asked Kimitsu to explain esoteric breathing some more.

I always do my "aah" breathing just before I go to sleep each day. Just one or two minutes is enough.

And the connection with the esoteric symbol in your plastic veil and start line drawings (figures 3.7 and 3.9)?

Beyond the language! Beyond the idea conception!

I asked who taught him Buddhism.

I first got interested in Buddhism by reading a German and an Englishman—Hermann Beckh and Christmas Humphries. They turned me into a Tibetan Buddhism maniac. Beckh's book came flying to me. One day when I was past my fiftieth birthday, I was standing in front of the Kotobuki Labor Center and they were throwing out some un-needed books from the reading room they have there. In amongst the discarded books was Beckh's *Buddhism*. It was a paperback Japanese translation in two volumes. It was one of three books I found in the pile of discards from the reading room that I wanted to read. Some Shakespeare research . . . a book on Sino-American relations... and Hermann Beckh.

Somehow the conversation got on to George Orwell.

His works have an idealistic, utopian streak. But his feet are always planted firmly on the ground. His writings are firmly grounded in experience. And he looks at the world from a worker's perspective. He's got it right. The human race is not making some kind of Darwinian progression—it's actually regressing. I respect him for his experience. Shot in the neck in the Spanish civil war. *1984* is his masterpiece. Just as good as Arthur C. Clarke's *2001*. The key word is "telescreen." A life with no privacy. The dictator can see everything you do. Centralized authority. *Central power, central heating.* There are a lot of surveillance cameras in our society today. I don't mind having them around the Diet building, but it's wrong to put them up in shopping districts like Ginza or Shibuya. I mean—if crime were to be completely eliminated, people wouldn't be able to make detective movies or crime novels any more. Crime and gangs are part of culture, and they have their own nobility. Trying to crush them totally—that's fascism. A merciful spirit, compassion—that's the most necessary thing in a ruler.

So you don't want the cops to arrest those guys who stole your wallet?

I certainly do want them arrested. They're like bacteria or a virus, and the challenge is how to eradicate them. Thinking in terms of human karma, someone who causes other people to suffer should go to hell one time and practice austerities there. That hell doesn't necessarily have to be a prison. It can be a guilty conscience within oneself. Jack the Ripper, the Suffolk strangler, the Rostov Ripper,[75] Hitler, Eichmann . . . I want them to suffer, even if it's after they've died.

Hell does exist, you know. Cause and effect is a law of nature. If you kill someone, you will be punished. In America they've got the death penalty, and I've got no problem with that. Because it is in harmony with the great law of nature. If you tried to apply humanism to American society, the whole system would collapse.

But what about that stuff just now about the importance of leaders showing mercy?

Criminals are an exception. If you kill someone, you have to die. After all—you are human, therefore you have self-responsibility. We're not animals you know. We're not monkeys at Noge Zoo.[76]

It's probably true, what Shintarō Ishihara says about Chinese having criminal DNA. I mean—just look at their lifestyle. They eat snakes and civets! With a national character like that, it's hardly surprising if they murder and rob. They celebrate New Year by eating cobras, you know!

That is discrimination!

Not at all. Hey—do you know how they greet each other? "Hi there—eaten any snakes today? No? Well I've got a nice cobra at my place, so I'll bring it over!"

Don't be ridiculous.

No, I'm perfectly serious. I heard it from a Chinese docker. You should do some fieldwork on this. I'm not saying they're savages. I'm just saying that they do have that kind of tradition. Only in the south, mind. Canton, Hong Kong. Because there are lots of crocodiles and other tropical animals in southern China.

Well I've heard that down in your native Kyushu it is not unknown for people to eat exotic foods, including snakes . . .

No way! Kyushu people are civilized, and besides, there's plenty of rice, so they don't need to eat snakes and things.

Well either way, there is surely no connection between people's dietary practices and their propensity to commit crime.

Oh, yes, there is a connection. China's got a huge population, and there are Chinatowns all over the world. But I'm not saying Chinese people are bad. It's actually we Japanese who are bad. We're always after speed and guns. People make a big fuss about human rights, but this kind of thing really has to be cracked down on hard.

I told Kimitsu he was too drunk and talking nonsense. He should go back to his room and get some sleep.

People sleep. And when they sleep, they dream. Flying through the sky or something.

Figure 3.10. "Horrable" scene.

Kimitsu sometimes draws some quite surrealistic scenes. One day I brought an old sketch pad with me to the Apollo Café to see if he'd like to draw something. I hadn't noticed that there was one page, right at the back of the pad, that already had a drawing on it. It was a copy drawn seven years earlier by my son, eleven years old at the time, of a "Far Side" cartoon by Gary Larson. In the cartoon a man and a cow are sharing a small lifeboat after surviving a shipwreck. They have run out of food. The man is thinking of killing the cow and turning it into a steak. The cow is hoping that the man might start decaying so that grass would grow off his body. Kimitsu spotted the drawing and embellished it. Now the little lifeboat is threatened by a US marine officer with a bazooka, concealed under the water and breathing through a long air tube (like those prisoners who escaped up the Vistula River in one of Kimitsu's Movietone memories). Apparently mistaking the man and cow for the Soviet navy, he takes aim—"rock (lock) on target"—*while shouting* "Kozack (Cossack) busted (bastard) bitch! Peath (peace) breaker!" *Sensing danger, the cow tells the man:* "Something else behind your back." *The man cynically replies* "what brady (bloody, i.e., bloody stupid) talk." *Someone, perhaps the artist, more urgently warns,* "Be carefull under the watar!" (Be careful, there is something dangerous under the water). *A passing octopus, identified as* "military analist Redell Hart" (Basil Liddell Hart) *pours a despairing plume of black ink into the ocean and observes,* "Nothing I can say analysing about this horrable scene."

Thus a relatively innocent (if somewhat bizarre) cartoon is transformed into yet another riff on Kimitsu's obsession with warfare and the impressive but frightening power of the Americans. It is an ominous moment with death imminent, yet retains some of the black humor of Larson's original.

The Fourteenth Conversation

June 10, 2007

A sullen, darkly cloudy day in the rainy season, with thundery showers from the morning. Today I brought with me a professional physicist—Norikazu Todoroki, a young research fellow at Kanagawa University.[77] *He kindly agreed to discuss Kimitsu's use of terms from quantum physics and thermodynamics that were over my head. He helped me with some of the footnotes in this narrative. But I started by asking Kimitsu about his admiration for Shin'ichi Nakazawa. He often praised Nakazawa for having spent three years training with Buddhist monks in Tibet, but while I appreciated Kimitsu's stress on the need for theory to be grounded in experience, surely that in itself was not enough to make Nakazawa a great culture hero. What else impressed Kimitsu about him? At first Kimitsu just laughed at this question, but when I pressed him he finally responded:*

I respect Nakazawa sensei for his thought—it is thought born of experience. He honed his body, he sharpened his mind—brilliant. He started with image training.[78] That was his basic training if you like, like mine when I was in the SDF. (They do image training in the army too, you know—and in yakuza gangs. Target practice, virtual training.) That way Nakazawa shed his skin, like a snake or a cicada. He was reborn. The first time you get born out of a woman. The second time you get born in the form of achieving enlightenment.

Kimitsu started drawing figure 3.11 (below). Starting with the bubble with an arrow pointing to the woman, and working anti-clockwise, the Japanese captions read "lightness/heaviness of karma," "cosmic egg," "Nakazawa" (i.e., Kimitsu's guru, Shin'ichi Nakazawa), "immature = egg," "10, 20, 30, 40, 50 years," "second birth!"

Figure 3.11. Rebirth.

The cosmic egg in the diagram is an idea I took from Deleuze and Guattari.[79] We get born from the cosmic egg but remain immature; we suffer and undergo training for ten, twenty or thirty years, and then we have a second birth! Although there are some people who achieve enlightenment as soon as they're born. I expect that's how it was with Shin'ichi Nakazawa. In my own case, I haven't got there yet. It's a process that depends on how heavy or light your karma is. And when you achieve enlightenment, you go back to the woman. We are part of the universe, but at the same time we are creating the universe (*Guffaw*).

Todoroki: Susumu Nishibe, the Tokyo University professor who recommended Nakazawa for a position there and then resigned in protest when the appointment was rejected, is well known for his political conservatism, but what is Nakazawa's political position?

Buddhism and Communism don't mix particularly well. But Nakazawa is universal, unique, and neither left nor right. When Professor Nakazawa appears on TV, he talks in a detached way about myths and things. He uses ancient stories to illuminate present-day issues. He uses metaphor. I always sense that he has achieved enlightenment from the way he talks. I've been especially impressed by his willingness to criticize Japanese Buddhism. To use a metaphor from physics, there is too much extensive quantity (*gaienryō*, see note 60 of this chapter) in Japanese Buddhism. There's too much rubbish in the way. It's a symplectic manifold. An object in the middle of the vector.

Todoroki: He seems to be adapting these scientific terms to mean things like money, sex and prestige that are barriers to enlightenment.

As in Hegelian dialectics, it rises. When you go up you find the world of the Buddha, the world of the Bodhisattvas, the world of enlightenment. But if you go sideways you end up in hell, the world of the Asura.[80] As Marx says, the dialectical vector rises while moving left and right, and finally reaches enlightenment. But if you are weighed down with rubbish like women, money, or vanity, you cannot reach enlightenment. That is what I call extensive quantity, or rubbish. It's all there in Nakazawa!

*He drew a diagram on the back of our café bill. It showed an arrow moving vertically upward while frenetically moving back and forth horizontally. It had "women," "money," and "appearances" stuck to the bottom of it like some kind of cement-like substance. Around the diagram, clockwise from bottom left, were written the words "symplectic manifold," (*sinpurekutikku tayōtai*) "lamina" (*yōsōtai*), "extensive quantity" (*gaienryō*), "hell" (*jigoku*), "dialectical" (*benshōhōteki*) and "hard-working farmer" (*tokunōka*; this may have related to a different conversation).*

*Pressed to explain further, Kimitsu produced another drawing. This time Adolf Eichmann was attempting to reach enlightenment but was being held back by the Jewish people he had killed (figure 3.12). Clockwise from the left, the notes on it read "MASS," "one tensor" (*ichi no tensoru*), "karma" (*gyō [karuma]*), "bad karma" (*akugō*), "extensive quantity" (*gaienryō*) "principle of cause and effect" (*inga no rihō*), and "good karma" (*zengō*).*

Figure 3.12. Eichmann's karma.

The principle of cause and effect is precisely as stated by David Hume.[81] In this diagram Eichmann has committed such terrible sins that he cannot achieve enlightenment without undergoing terrible suffering. A shame, because Eichmann was a good man in his youth. He was a handsome military officer, attractive to women. There were a lot like him among the Nazis. Good lookers. If the dialectic had gone to the right, he might have done good deeds, but Eichmann turned to the left and did bad deeds. A negative feedback bootstrap, that was.[82]

As I was about to leave, Kimitsu reached into his shirt pocket and pulled out a five thousand yen note. It was a first installment on repayment of a 15,000 yen loan he had asked for some months ago after his wallet was lost or stolen (see p. 34 above; I'd subsequently lent him another 5,000.) He never quite finished repaying his loans, but he did try.

Afterwards, I asked Todoroki san what he thought about Kimitsu's use of mathematics and physics—"extensive quantity," "symplectic manifold," "tensor field," "bootstrap," etc. After careful consideration, Todoroki san concluded that Kimitsu's usage bore no recognizable resemblance to the meaning of these terms in mathematics or physics, though they might work for him on a strictly metaphorical level. Further reading convinced me that these terms were mostly taken from Shin'ichi Nakazawa, who has himself been accused by his critics of abusing mathematical terminology in his philosophical writings. By the time Kimitsu has put his own spin on Nakazawa's terms, they are so far removed from their original mathematical meaning that it probably does not matter too much if one does not fully understand that original meaning. Sometime in the late 1990s or early 2000s, Kimitsu fell under the spell of Nakazawa, doubtless admiring his use of exotic scientific terminology, his ambitious attempt to fuse natural and social science, and the cachet of those three years in Tibet.

The Fifteenth Conversation

August 13, 2007

I had been trying to find a publisher for the Conversations; four different publishers had turned the manuscript down. It was my last chance to talk with Kimitsu and somehow strengthen the manuscript before I departed for an eight-month spell in America. I didn't know if Kimitsu would be alive when I got back to Yokohama. I wanted to fill a few holes in the narrative while I still could.

You talked a lot more about your father than about your mother. Any particular reason?

When all's said and done, I guess I'm a matrilineal kind of guy. In Japan men are weak and women are strong. Women are particularly strong west of

Nagoya. It's a matrilineal society. Empress Suiko,[83] Princess Nukata,[84] Eva Peron.

Was your family "matrilineal"?

Oh yes. My mother graduated from a women's normal school[85] which is now the education faculty of Kumamoto University, and became an elementary school teacher. There were always lots of school books lying around our house. They had lots of illustrations—the Saint Bartholomew's Day Massacre,[86] that kind of thing. She was the daughter of a wealthy farming family.

My father didn't have much to say for himself, and when he came home drunk he'd have his futon laid out for him and he'd go to sleep. He was a quiet man. I liked my father, so I always used to wonder if he wouldn't come home a little earlier. I found it hard to get on with my mother. She was a bit too cultured for me.

When I was in the SDF, I went home for New Year one time, got drunk, and said "mum, I've been with a woman from Susukino!" She gave me a real stinging slap. "Proper cultured people don't go to places like that." Thinking about it afterwards I realized she was quite right, and I stopped going. That was real mother-child communication, so I felt, sort of, persuaded. By chance my father was not present at the time, so I never told him about all this. But after that, if Hirakawa-kun or Takagi-kun said "come on, let's go to Susukino!"—I'd decline the invitation. That was an interface for me, the moment I crossed the border from childhood to adulthood. My relationship with my mother wasn't particularly damaged by the incident. She had what Tetsuro Watsuji[87] calls a "typhoon character"—she'd fly into a rage, but she'd soon calm down and she didn't bear grudges.

(*Changing the subject*) The only thing that's going to make this world peaceful is an invasion by extra-terrestrials. A common enemy, that's what we need. Just look at what happened in the old Yugoslavia. As long as dangerous enemies like Hitler and Stalin were around, all the different ethnic minorities managed to work together, but the moment those enemies were gone, it descended into civil war. The same principle governs the entire world.

I often went travelling with my father. We went to Mount Kirishima, Mount Aso, looking for the sources of rivers etc. We went to look at the army air-arm training ground at Kikuchi. They had these old-fashioned biplanes there—this was before the air-raids started. We often watched the youth corps doing their training. (My two younger brothers were too small to be taken along.) When you're hiking or mountain climbing, there's no stress, so you can talk.

Because my father worked for a bank, we used to get a lot of cabinet information sent our way, and photo-magazines to do with the war. They always had pictures of Hitler, Mussolini or Tōjō on the cover. General Yamashita accepting General Percival's surrender after the fall of Singapore. Naturally I was affected by all that. To a degree I was a militaristic little boy. But unlike a lot of other people, I didn't just flip to being anti-government after the war ended.

What do you think of Prime Minister Abe and his stress on patriotism? Do you consider yourself a patriot? Do you have any feeling for the national flag and anthem?

Abe lacks experience. He should go and practice Buddhist austerities in Tibet. Japanese Buddhism is shit. Korean Buddhism's not much good either. Tibet is good. The five elements.[88] Mercy, peace, the mantra.

What are you reading these days?

Mathematics. Richard Feynman. Light and material. It's intellectual. Light, particles. In his experiment when he passed light through a slit, the light that struck the observer's eye was perceived as black (being aware of the slit), but light is not like that—its movement continues eternally. The connection between that and Tibetan Buddhism is that ordinary people who are bound by material desires can look at light and it will appear black. But if you interpret it in the light of Tibetan Buddhist praxis, you can get away from the Six Domains of the Desire Realm, like exceeding the speed of light. *Feynman discusses light, that goes through slits. It's an evergreen [=unchanging] light, but to the observer it seems to change color and slow down.* We are slow, and we live in a *painful world.* It's a problem of speed. The operating principle. A problem of the mind. The mind is like a mirror, and it creates various images. One feels attachment to another. When you feel attachment to something, light becomes black.

NOTES

1. I have not been able to find the quotation to which Kimitsu refers, though it may be derived from Chesterton's essay, "Sincerity and the Gallows" in his book *What's Wrong with the World* (1910).
2. Far Eastern Network. This used to be the name of the U.S. military radio service in Japan.
3. Kun—a slightly rougher, more masculine suffix than "san."
4. The famous all-women drama troupe based in the town of Takarazuka, Hyogo prefecture. Most of the big stars are women who play glamorous male roles.
5. Chan—an even more familiar, jocular suffix than "kun." Not normally used for names of cabinet ministers.

6. This notorious pork-barrel politician proved that he did have a conscience after all by killing himself just a few months after this conversation, in connection with a shameful financial scandal. It was the first time in post-war Japanese history that a serving cabinet minister had committed suicide.

7. Nationalistic maverick LDP politician, born in Dalian, Manchuria, but raised in Fukuoka.

8. Minister of Defense at the time of this interview. Hawkish. Born in Shimabara, Nagasaki prefecture. Forced to resign on July 3, 2007, following public outcry over a speech in which he stated that he now accepted that the atomic bombing of his native Nagasaki had been necessary to bring an end to the Pacific War.

9. Buddhist deity, protector of children and travelers.

10. Stopping trains have far fewer ticket inspections than express trains.

11. An alternative name for the Osaka doya-gai, Kamagasaki, which is located in Nishinari ward. So saying you are from Nishinari means that you are an impoverished day laborer.

12. Since article 9 of Japan's constitution states that "land, sea, and air forces, as well as other war potential, will never be maintained," the armed forces are called the Ground, Maritime and Air Self-Defence Forces (SDF).

13. Nanba is an Osaka entertainment district.

14. Monjayaki or pan-fried batter is actually considered a specialty of down-town Tokyo rather than Osaka.

15. Japan's biggest yakuza syndicate.

16. *Sankaku Kōen.* A famous Kamagasaki landmark, where many homeless men sleep.

17. Literally "unmovable rock"—this large, rather phallic outcrop of rock is a local landmark near Yamaga.

18. Lamb's most famous poem, "The Old Familiar Faces" is thought to have been written in 1798.

19. Had Kimitsu been a conventional Japanese person he would have bought the crackers in Yokohama, prior to setting out, since gifts taken on a visit are supposed to be a local specialty of the place one has come from.

20. Shaman-queen thought to have reigned over part of Japan in the third century CE. Revered by Kimitsu.

21. The Festival of the Dead, held in mid-August in most parts of Japan. A traditional time of year to visit family.

22. Very famous Taiwanese baseball player who had a brilliant career in Japan as a batting star of the Yomiuri Giants.

23. *Keshō no mono wa hito ni sugata ga mirenai tokoro ni kiete yuku.*

24. Shin'ichi Nakazawa (b. 1950). Controversial Buddhism scholar and critic; head of the Institut pour la Science Sauvage (Yasei no Kagaku Kenkyūjo) at Meiji University. Author of the best-selling *Chibetto no Mōtsaruto* (The Mozart of Tibet; 1983) and many other widely read works. Heavily criticized in the media for defending the Aum Shinrikyō cult even after its nerve-gas attack on the Tokyo subway in 1995. As far as I know it is only Kimitsu who refers to him as "guru." Kimitsu's devotion to Nakazawa was the biggest change I noticed in his intellectual interests between the 1990s and the 2000s. It was striking that I could never get him to mention another Japanese writer who impressed or influenced him. All his other heroes were European or American, though often he would find traces of Oriental-style thought in their works.

25. Colin Wilson (b. 1931). British thinker, novelist, student of the occult. He made a major contribution to British existentialism with his seminal work, *The Outsider*, published in 1956 when he was just 24.

26. From 1849 to 1854, Dostoevsky was confined in a forced labor camp in the Siberian city of Omsk. On the basis of that experience he wrote *The House of the Dead* (1862). In this work Dostoevsky uses the forced labor camp as a metaphor for the whole of Russian society, and this may well have influenced Kimitsu's idea of Kotobuki as a concentration camp without walls (p. 6 above).

27. Francis Chichester (1901–1972). First yachtsman to sail around the world solo (1966–1967). Author of *The Lonely Sea and the Sky*.

28. Robin Knox-Johnston (b. 1937). First yachtsman to sail around the world solo and non-stop (1968–1969; Chichester had made one port call, at Sydney).

29. Paul Kammerer (1880–1926). Austrian biologist, a Lamarckian who claimed to have demonstrated the inheritance of acquired characteristics in experiments with toads etc. Accused by Bateson (1861–1926) and others of unethical research methods, he subsequently killed himself.

30. George Orwell (1903–1950). In 1949 Orwell handed over a list of people he considered Communists to the British government and was later accused of betraying some of his friends.

31. In 1998 historian David Cesarani published a biography of Koestler, *Arthur Koestler: The Homeless Mind*, which accused him of being a serial rapist, among other things.

32. *Taishōsei.* The topic of Nakazawa's 2004 paper, *Taishōsei Jinruigaku: Kaie Sōbāji V* (Symmetrical Anthropology: Cahiers Sauvages V).

33. Takeda is a well-loved Japanese actor, best known for his role as an amiable school teacher in the long-running television drama *Kinpachi Sensei*. He was born in 1949, nine years later than Kimitsu and four years after the war ended.

34. I could never get a clear word from Kimitsu as to whether his father quit Yasuda Bank, or was fired. His account varies between the two.

35. A famous Japanese poet, born 1931.

36. Very long series of films and TV dramas about an Edo era law-man who wanders the country incognito, meting out justice to evil-doers.

37. One of Kimitsu's favorite words is "*omoshiro-okashii*"—literally, "interesting and funny"—with the "funny" somewhere in between funny peculiar and funny ha-ha.

38. In Japanese *kun* is normally used only with male names. It is sometimes applied to women who play male roles on stage, and to striptease artistes etc. Kimitsu humorously applies it to the other girls in Yamaga who did not go on to become male-role actors like Kōzuki.

39. I have changed her name to protect her privacy.

40. Kimitsu was referring to two fossilized skeletons that were dug up at an archaeological site near Mantua, northern Italy, on February 5, 2007. Kimitsu's explanation is of course speculative, but they were male and female, did appear to be in an embrace, and arrowheads and a knife were among the artifacts found with them. Mantua is near to the setting of Shakespeare's *Romeo and Juliet*, which encouraged romantic speculation at the time.

41. October 21, 1600. This was the decisive battle in which Ieyasu Tokugawa defeated his rivals among the regents of the late Hideyoshi Toyotomi, paving the way for the birth of the Tokugawa shogunate. It was a very significant battle, perhaps indeed a once-in-a-hundred-year event.

42. I cannot seem to trace this film. *Operation Mad Ball* (1957) sounds right, but it stars Jack Lemmon and Mickey Rooney rather than George Peppard.

43. Slightly obscure . . . perhaps a reference to the hostesses at bars where some of the drinking went on.

44. Kimitsu said this in English; it is a literal translation of the Japanese expletive "*bakayarō*."

45. Lieutenant General LaVern E. Weber. He was based at Makomanai in the early 1950s, during the Korean War.

46. The term autopoiesis was, as Kimitsu said, invented by Humberto Maturana, (b. 1928) and his student Francisco Varela (1946–2001), a pair of Chilean biologist-philosophers, in their seminal text, *Autopoiesis and Cognition* (1980). A Japanese translation was published in 1991. Valera defines autopoiesis thus: "The process whereby an organization produces itself. An autopoietic organization is an autonomous and self-maintaining unity which contains component-producing processes. The components, through their interaction, generate recursively the same network of processes which produced them. An autopoietic system is operationally closed and structurally state determined with no apparent inputs and outputs. A cell, an organism, and perhaps a corporation are examples of autopoietic systems." http://pespmc1.vub.ac.be/ASC/autopoiesis.html. (I could never quite figure out the connection between affordance, autopoiesis and Armageddon in Kimitsu's discourse, but I thought he might possibly be on to something.)

47. David Bohm (1917–1992). American quantum physicist.

48. David Koresh (1959–1993). Founder of the Branch Davidians. He and 78 of his followers were killed by officers of the FBI and ATE during a 51-day siege of the cult's ranch at Waco, Texas.

49. Karel Čapek (1890–1938). Czech writer who invented the word 'robot.'

50. Eric Hoffer, author of *Working and Thinking on The Waterfront* (1969, Japanese translation 1992).

51. Referencing Victorian folklorist Sir James Fraser—probably quite obscure for Vinnie.

52. An incident of August 1, 1966. Whitman killed 16 people, including his wife and mother. About the same number were wounded.

53. November 12, 1966.

54. Chicago, July 14, 1966.

55. Ian Brady (b. 1938), Myra Hindley (1942–2002), known collectively as the Moors Murderers. They killed five children and buried the bodies on a moor in the north of England.

56. Christine Keeler. The model and call girl whose affair with war minister John Profumo while she was also seeing a Soviet spy brought down the Conservative government of Harold Macmillan in 1963.

57. Theoretical physicist, 1907–1981. In 1949 he became the first Japanese ever to win a Nobel Prize.

58. Bootstrap. It is of course impossible literally to "pull oneself up by one's bootstraps." Hence "bootstrapping" is a term used to signify doing things that appear logically impossible by one's own power. For example, how can a computer turn itself on, when it would appear to be incapable of doing anything in its off state? Hence one of the meanings of "bootstrapping"—usually shortened to "booting," or "rebooting" when done again—is the act of switching on a computer. Kimitsu, influenced by Shin'ichi Nakazawa, uses this term much more generally, to signify a system that creates or recreates itself.

59. In mathematics, a tensor is similar to a vector but applied to higher-order objects. "The modern component-free approach to the theory of a tensor views a tensor as an abstract object, expressing some definite type of multi-linear concept. . . . In differential geometry an intrinsic geometric statement may be described by a tensor field on a manifold, and then doesn't need to make reference to coordinates at all" (Wikipedia).

60. Extensive quantity. A term from physics, translating *gaienryō*, one of Kimitsu's favorite terms. It means kinds of quantity whose magnitude depends on the size (extension) of an entity, such as volume, mass and energy, as opposed to intensive quantities like density or pressure, which are not dependent on the size (extension) of an entity. The correct Japanese characters are外延量. Kimitsu wrote it as外縁量on the back of our bill at the Apollo Café, changing the meaning of the kanji from outside-extent-quantity to outside-connection-quantity. I guess that this is a simple error rather than an innovation, since Kimitsu has clearly got this term from Shin'ichi Nakazawa, who writes it in the conventional style. The term crops up in Nakazawa's *Philosophia Japonica* (2001). Kimitsu seems to use the term to mean anything extraneous to the spirit that holds it back from achieving enlightenment.

61. "In mathematics, a symplectic manifold is a smooth manifold, M, equipped with a closed, nondegenerate, skew-symmetric 2-form, ω, called the symplectic form" (Wikipedia). Another mathematical term played with by Shin'ichi Nakazawa in *Philosophia Japonica.*

62. Péter Frankl (b. 1953). Eccentric Hungarian mathematician, resident in Tokyo since 1988, who also does juggling in the street. Hardly a typical vagabond.

63. *Ressentiment*—a term used by Nietzsche to denote the hatred felt by the weak toward the strong.

64. Lucy Blackman, a British air hostess, was murdered in 2000. Jōji Obara, a naturalized Japanese of Korean descent, was accused of the crime but found not guilty in a court verdict handed down on April 24, 2007. I include Kimitsu's deeply racist comment merely for documentary completeness.

65. This was one of the job creation programs for day laborers run by the city of Tokyo. Like most of them, it paid a small wage (6,000 yen is about $60), and required little actual work. Going home after an hour or two was a common pattern.

66. At the time Hideki Matsui was batting for the New York Yankees and Daisuke Matsuzaka was pitching for the Boston Red Sox.

67. Leader of the Aum Shinrikyō cult, notorious for its sarin gas attack on the Tokyo subway, 1995. Sentenced to death and currently awaiting execution.

68. A large island off the south coast of South Korea, source of many of the Korean migrant workers in Kotobuki.

69. An unlucky year in Taoist cosmology, widely believed in Japan.

70. Austrian-Jewish Holocaust survivor who became a famous psychiatrist and neurologist.

71. Looking at statistics for the last 20 years, it seems that about 20–30,000 people go to prison each year in Japan. The prison population was under 50,000 when Kimitsu did his time, but has since risen to about 75,000. Each year about 3,000 students enter the University of Tokyo, with total enrolment about 15,000, so Kimitsu's humorous comparison is slightly inaccurate.

72. A.P. Elkin (1891–1979) was a highly influential Australian anthropologist. The Ildawongga are an aboriginal tribe of Western Australia. "They may have been the last of the free-living aborigines of Australia to come into Western contact" (Tindale's Catalogue of Australian Aboriginal Tribes, http://archives.samuseum.sa.gov.au/tindaletribes/ildawongga.htm). However, I cannot trace the Barthagen. Perhaps Kimitsu is thinking of one of the tribes living around Mount Hagen in Papua New Guinea.

73. Leprosy sufferers continued to be kept in forced confinement in Japan until 1996, although a vaccine to kill the leprosy bacterium was developed in 1952.

74. Kenji Miyazawa (1896–1933) is one of Japan's most celebrated modern poets. He died at the age of 37, of pneumonia rather than tuberculosis. Takuboku Ishikawa was also a poet; he died of TB at the age of 27.

75. The Suffolk (Ipswich) strangler: Steve Wright, convicted in 2008 of murdering five women in and around Ipswich, U.K. in 2006. The Rostov Ripper: Andrei Chikatilo, executed in 1994 after being convicted of killing fifty-three women and children, mainly in and around Rostov, Russia, 1978–1990.

76. A small zoo within walking distance of Kotobuki.

77. Now he has a tenured position at Chiba Industrial University.

78. In Japan, "image training" is a term mostly used in a sporting context. It means replacing negative images of failure with positive images of success.

79. Gilles Deleuze (1925–1975) and Pierre-Félix Guattari (1930–1992): French new-wave philosophers. The term "cosmic egg" was coined by astrophysicist Georges Lemaître (1894–1966) to denote the state of the universe just before the Big Bang. Deleuze and Guattari's contribution was to link this concept from astrophysics with cosmic eggs appearing in ancient myths from China, Egypt, India, etc.: "There is a fundamental convergence between science and myth, embryology and mythology, the biological egg and the psychic or cosmic egg"—Deleuze and Guattari, *A Thousand Plateaus* (1987), p. 164.

80. Japanese *Ashura*—demons in Buddhist and Hindu mythology.

81. David Hume (1711–1776) famously criticized simplistic attribution of cause-and-effect relations between consecutive events ("Post hoc, ergo propter hoc"), arguing that people can only perceive correlation, not causality. Kimitsu does not seem to be aware of this when he says that Hume stated the principle of cause and effect. Instead he seems to have a fairly simple notion that cause (sin) results in effect (punishment).

82. For "bootstrap," see note 58 above. In electronic engineering, negative feedback "occurs when the output of a system acts to oppose changes to the input of the system; with the result that the changes are attenuated" (Wikipedia). The term is also used metaphorically in psychology, economics, philosophy, etc. In Kimitsu's narrative, Eichmann's massacre of Jews has generated bad karma, which for Kimitsu is like a kind of negative radio wave preventing him from achieving enlightenment. An auspicious right-moving spiral would lead upward to enlightenment/heaven, but his deeds have sent him spiraling to the left and downward, towards something like hell.

83. Empress Suiko, 33rd emperor of Japan, reigned 593–628 CE. She was the first female emperor; there would be seven more, the last in the late eighteenth century. Today the rules of imperial succession officially exclude women, but this is a nineteenth-century innovation.

84. Princess Nukata (c. 630–690 CE). One of emperor Temmu's wives and a famous *waka* poet.

85. An old-fashioned name for a teacher training college.
86. A 1572 massacre of Huguenots by Catholics in Paris. Perhaps Kimitsu's mother taught at a protestant school.
87. Tetsuro Watsuji, 1889–1960. Philosopher. He argues that Japanese people have a "typhoon personality" in his famous book, *Fūdo* (1931; *Climate and Culture*, 1961).
88. Fire, wood, earth, metal, water. Compared with the European four elements, the Buddhist equivalent removes air and adds wood and metal.

Chapter Four

Kimitsu and Kotobuki to the Present Day

I went to California to do fieldwork in August 2007, wondering as usual whether I would ever see Kimitsu again. While in America, I was unable to discuss the matter with Kimitsu. He has no telephone. I sent him a picture postcard from Santa Barbara, but he later denied any knowledge of it.

In March 2008, I returned to Japan. My house was rented out until June, so for three months I lived in a doya in Kotobuki myself. The town is not as bad as its reputation. There were Chinese exchange students as well as welfare recipients living in my doya. I found Kimitsu in surprisingly good shape. I saw him a few times, but somehow we didn't do anything more with the manuscript. I had a lot of things on my mind at the university. It was nice to relax and talk about life with Kimitsu without having to write it all down and worry about whether it made sense. We went to the karaoke a couple of times. Kimitsu mostly sang sentimental ballads from Kyushu, plus *I Left My Heart in San Francisco*. He liked San Francisco because it was a port city.

In mid-June I returned to my own house. I still went for a drink with Kimitsu now and again. He never mentioned the manuscript unless I did. "We must do something about it," I would say. "Nah, no one's going to publish that piece of crap," he would reply. That was kind of sad. When we were working on it, he used to talk wistfully about making one more nostalgic trip down to Yamaga, this time with his published book in hand and his exotic English professor friend in tow. That would be quite a surprise for his older sister, the retired kindergarten principle, who'd always thought he was a complete failure. I enjoyed imagining that moment too. But now Kimitsu seemed to have cast that dream away. Buddhist renunciation, perhaps. On most occasions, he was in cheerful good spirits—surprisingly good spirits for an old man living out his twilight years in a filthy flophouse in almost total isolation.

Then I received word from my employers that I would be granted a one-year sabbatical in 2010–2011. The only condition was that I had to spend it abroad. I quickly made arrangements to spend it at the Nissan Institute in Oxford.

Suddenly, it was 2007 all over again. I was determined to improve the manuscript and find a publisher before I left Japan again. I rented out my house again and moved back to temporary digs in Kotobuki. I went to Kimitsu's room—room 111 at the Tokugawa-sō. He was out. He was out the next couple of times I called too. I asked the concierge of the Tokugawa-sō if he knew anything. He said Kimitsu was in hospital, and likely to stay there for quite a while. He did not know which hospital, but I made inquiries and traced him to the Red Cross Hospital at Shin-Yamashita. He'd had a stroke on December 13, 2009, while shopping in a convenience store. He had been lucky, in a sense—if it had happened when he was in his room he'd have died and the body might not have been found for weeks.

Kimitsu was very weak, confined to bed, and paralyzed down his left side. His speech was slurred, stumbling, and barely comprehensible. He would forget what he was saying halfway through a sentence. However, he had not lost his long-term memory. For instance, I asked if he was aware that Claude Lévi-Strauss had died at the age of 100. He said: "structural anthropology will never be the same again."

I visited him several times in hospital. The Japanese welfare system was looking after him very well. It paid all his bills during a four-month hospitalization. He was well cared for by kind nurses and even the food was quite good. After a month in an emergency ward he was moved to another hospital that took charge of his rehabilitation program. Eventually they had him walking about fairly steadily after he had been totally immobilized by the stroke.

The first time I visited him in hospital, I asked him if there was anything I could get him. He mimed smoking a cigarette and knocking back a drink. Both those activities were, of course, forbidden. However, on my next visit, I brought him a can of 0% alcohol beer. The moment he saw it a gleam came into his eye. He snatched it from me with his right hand (he had very little use of his left) and drank it down in several noisy gulps. Two minutes later he wet himself—the drink had gone straight through. I felt very stupid and had to call a nurse to change his nappy.

One small problem with Japanese hospitals is that they make you pay to watch TV. Kimitsu never seemed to have any of the 1,000-yen pre-paid cards needed to watch the TV at his bedside, and he said he had no money to buy any. So I bought him a couple of cards, and asked the duty nurse if she would look after a few thousand yen to pay for more. She was surprised at the request, since it turned out Kimitsu had plenty of money, brought to the hospital by his social welfare care worker, which was kept for him in a brown envelope with notes on the back detailing expenditure. It included several items for TV cards. Apparently he had totally forgotten about this, or possibly was trying through a deranged cunning to acquire even more TV cards. They did not do him much good anyway—they were worth 800 minutes of viewing, but he would fall asleep with the TV on and get through them in a night or so. I did sit with him to watch Japan play China at football on the night of February 6, 2010, and he correctly diagnosed a lack of shape and flow in the Japan team's play. It ended 0-0.

Several times I took my notebook computer with me when I visited, still hoping to strengthen the manuscript, but Kimitsu's voice was so slurred and halting that he could not communicate more than a few basic things. Another thing that gave grounds for hope was that Kimitsu kept up his sketching in hospital. The last sketch of Kimitsu's that I saw before leaving Japan showed one of his trademark Nazi officers, with an unpleasant sneer on his face, and with Kimitsu's own name written over the top. He had pinned it to the curtain around his hospital bed, like a sort of name plate.

I left Japan on March 30, 2010; Kimitsu left hospital on April 19. For four months he had eaten sensible food and drunk no alcohol. I rang up the hospital from Oxford on the morning of his departure and managed to get through to him. I urged him to stay on the wagon, since a return to his usual drinking habits would surely be the end of him. He said he was determined to do that, though when I'd asked him in hospital whether he would go back on the bottle, he'd laconically said "probably."

Three days before he left hospital, my friend Manami (now my second wife) visited him. He was able to engage in simple conversation. He asked her to lend him 2,000 yen, which he didn't need and was probably a randomly chosen sum of money. She gave him the money. He promised to pay her back after leaving hospital.

In June of that year, Manami went to visit Kimitsu at his room in the Tokugawa-sō. It had been kept ready for him. He was being seen daily by a care worker who kept him clean and had even cleaned up his room—a labor comparable to Hercules's cleaning of the Augean stables. But Manami could not be optimistic about Kimitsu's mental state . . . he seemed confused and unable to hold up a conversation.

When I returned from Britain in April 2011, I was distracted by the 3/11 disasters in north-eastern Japan, which I have been studying ever since. When I found time to look for Kimitsu at the Tokugawa-sō, he had left. The concierge knew only that he seemed to have gone to a different doya. For half a year, I was completely out of touch. Then I thought of ringing the welfare authorities for Naka-ku, the central ward of Yokohama where Kotobuki is located. They knew of him, and he was still alive. They could not tell me his whereabouts, due to the obsession with privacy that has pervaded

Japan in recent years. But a few days later I received a call from a caseworker, sitting in Kimitsu's room and using his mobile phone. He put Kimitsu on, and Kimitsu was very pleased to speak to me again. I learned that while I was in England, he'd suffered a second stroke. After another spell in hospital, he had been moved to a better doya and was now being looked after by the social services. Thus I obtained his new address, at a doya called the San'ei Kaikan. Soon after, I paid a visit.

The San'ei Kaikan is a modern, 9-story building in the center of Kotobuki, clad in light-blue tiles. It is one of many newly-built doya designed to house welfare recipients. It is run by a semi-governmental welfare corporation (*shakai fukushi hōjin*) called the Yokohama City Welfare Association (*Yokohama-shi Fukushi Kyōkai*). It is a very common pattern in Japanese social welfare policy for services to be entrusted to a variety of non-profits known collectively as "external bodies" (*gaikaku dantai*) of the city government, under the auspices of the Social Welfare Council (*Shakai Fukushi Kyōgikai*, or *Shakyō* for short). These are independent bodies, but most of their funding comes from city or prefectural governments, in the form of payments for provision of "entrusted services" (*itaku jigyō*). In recent years the proportion of welfare recipients has increased still further in Kotobuki, recently standing at 83%,[1] and a network of welfare corporations and non-profit organizations has developed to service the welfare population.

This is only one part of the transformation that has come over Kotobuki on its way to becoming a giant welfare center. When I arrived in Kotobuki in 1993, there were 87 doya. Today there are 122. Many of them have been built in the last few years, specifically to house welfare recipients. Some of them are outside the boundaries of what has traditionally been known as the Kotobuki district, making it harder to define the Kotobuki population. Including outlying doya raises the population from about 6,300 to over 8,000. These new doya have electric elevators—something quite unthinkable in a traditional doya. They have air-conditioning in every room, and some of them have showers on the ground floor or in the basement. A few even have one or two baths.

But some things never change. However well-appointed the new doya may be, they are still very cramped—typically a three-mat room, so about five square meters, with no shower, toilet, or even a wash-basin. Originally designed as cheap hotels, they have room rents which are cheap by hotel standards, but surprisingly expensive compared to low-end rental units. They charge 2,000 to 2,500 yen a night, which converts to 60,000 to 75,000 yen a month, enough to get a small apartment with your own kitchen, toilet, and bathroom in many parts of Yokohama.

These rents are now paid mostly by the city welfare authorities, who have to make special exceptions to the upper limit on rent payable by the livelihood protection system in order to meet the price set by the doya landlords.[2]

It is a slightly murky arrangement, but it has several advantages to the welfare authorities. First, doya do not charge any deposit (*shikikin*) or key money (*reikin*). These initial payments can be substantial in Japan—there is much variation, but one not uncommon pattern is two months' rent for deposit, two more for key money (a non-returnable gift to the landlord), plus a sum equivalent to another month's worth of rent payable to the realtor who introduces the property, and the first month's rent in advance. That adds up to half a year's rent, and these items are specifically excluded from the scope of livelihood protection. Second, doya do not require a personal guarantor, unlike most private landlords. The need for a guarantor has long been a stumbling block to official efforts to house homeless people, who seldom have a respectable friend with a steady job willing to vouch for good behavior and be personally liable for rent arrears. Third, many of the other people living in Kotobuki are also on welfare, so there is no local objection to welfare recipients moving into the district—unlike most residential areas of Japanese cities, where NIMBY objections to welfare recipients being housed locally may be expected. And fourth, many of the people put on welfare in Kotobuki have lived there before, have friends there, know the place and feel at home there.

Thus the practice of paying over the odds to house elderly welfare recipients in tiny rooms in a notorious slum district is not quite as bizarre as it appears at first glance, though anyone would admit that there is room for discussion.

With that in mind, join me as I pay my first visit in nearly two years to Kimitsu Nishikawa. It is late summer 2011 and I have just succeeded in acquiring his address.

I explain my business to the concierge, sitting behind his reinforced glass screen at the reception. He eyes me with suspicion, but lets me in after I sign my name in the visitor's book. I take the elevator, sharing it with an old man in a wheelchair and his case-worker. The elevator smells of disinfectant and has a prominent sign saying NO SPITTING. I get out at the fifth floor, and turn left down the corridor. I walk past a long row of anonymous green doors, very close to each other reflecting the smallness of the rooms. I come to the last one on the left. It is the only one with a name plate on the door: 510 西川紀光.

Norimitsu Nishikawa. I have gradually realized that this is how everybody pronounces his name. Despite his insistence that he hates being called "Norimitsu" because of the name's association with the emperor system, it seems to be just me who calls him "Kimitsu."

The reason he has a name plate is to stop him from wandering into other people's rooms by mistake. They say he has mild dementia. For a similar reason, his door has no key. He always loses keys, and since he has no valuables worth stealing, it makes sense to leave his room unlocked.

Very well—let us push open the door, saying his name as we enter.

"Kimitsu?"

His living environment has greatly changed. Gone are the cobwebs, the cockroaches, the fetid smell. This room is clean, with a working air-conditioner, TV, and an aluminum-frame bed like the ones in hospitals bed. His clothes are hung neatly on pegs, his personal possessions stored in a wall cupboard.

The other thing that immediately strikes me about the room is the complete absence of books and journals.

It is mid-afternoon, but the curtains are drawn and the TV is on in the darkened room. Ladies' volleyball. And lying inert on his hospital bed is Kimitsu Nishikawa.

He makes no movement as I enter the room.

"Kimitsu?"

He stirs slightly.

"Mister Tom?"

"Kimitsu, how are you?"

"Pretty damn bad, thank you."

Two strokes in three years have taken their toll. He has also developed early-stage liver cancer, and has recently undergone a surgical procedure in which a catheter was inserted into his body to apply medicine to the liver. The stroke has left him with almost no use of his left arm, and his speech is soft and slurred even when sober—which he always is, these days. But listening carefully, I realize that what he says still makes sense. And as we converse, I gather that he is still able to get about on his own, making his own way to the day center where he has his baths and haircuts. And to him it is very important that he has not been institutionalized, but still has his own room and the freedom to come and go as he pleases.

The books are a sad loss. He tells me they disappeared somehow, around the time he was moved from his old doya to the present one. Much later, I have a conversation with the head of the care team, in which he admits that he authorized the destruction of Kimitsu's book collection at that time. "They took up a lot of space," he apologetically observes, "and they were getting moldy. Some of them had insects living in them."

Kimitsu has also been deprived of his booze. Under an agreement he assented to with his doctor, Hiroko Tsuchiya of the Kotobuki-chō Clinic, he lives a cashless existence. She argued that if Kimitsu had cash, he would use it to buy alcohol. He would then start drinking again, likely leading to a third stroke and death. Unable to deny the logic of that, Kimitsu reluctantly consented to what he calls her "siege strategy." His meals are delivered to his room three times a day, and he gets a bath four times a week at the day-care center. A care worker comes three times a week to clean his room and once a week she takes his clothes to the laundry. If he wants for anything other than alcohol, his caseworker takes him shopping, using Kimitsu's social welfare cash, which is kept for him by the management of the care team. He is not allowed to have cash if the care worker is not with him.

The fact is, Kimitsu is not a reformed alcoholic; probably he never will be. He always wants a drink. One time I took him to a cheap Chinese restaurant in the neighborhood. I ordered a bowl of noodles, he ordered a glass of shōchū.

"Sorry," I told the owner of the restaurant, "he's not allowed alcohol. Please give him a glass of oolong tea." The owner complied. The next time he was near our table, Kimitsu said "boy, do me a favor and put a shot of shōchū in this." Again I had to sadly shake my head to countermand the order. He was downcast. It was hard.

Another time I took him to a family restaurant called Gusto with some of my students. I ordered him a glass of tea. One of the students was late and I had to walk to the station and collect her. By the time I got back to the restaurant, Kimitsu was on his second high-ball. He had told the students it was quite OK and got them to place the order.

I had to scold everybody when I got back to Gusto. "I wish I was addicted to fruit-juice, rather than alcohol," Kimitsu told the students wistfully. "I don't really like fruit juice, so it wouldn't be too hard to not drink it." I pointed out that if he was a fruit-juice addict he'd be dying for a glass of fruit-juice rather than saké. "Oh yes—I hadn't thought of that," he sarcastically replied.

As these incidents show, Kimitsu deeply resents his forced sobriety at one level. At another level, however, he understands it. Let us say that his head understands, even if his heart does not. He knows that without the intervention of Dr. Tsuchiya and the care team, he would probably be dead by now. And that is not something he has ever wished for. Some men in Kotobuki drink in a literally suicidal style, unable to stop until forced to do so by illness or lack of cash. But Kimitsu was always a controlled alcoholic. He knew he required alcohol like a car requires gasoline, and he took steps to make sure he could always get it. He kept accounts. After he went on welfare, he made sure he had enough cash left on the last day of the month to buy four or five one-cups of the cheapest saké from a nearby vending machine. When I had first met him he had mainly been drinking shōchū, a considerably stronger kind of liquor, but he deliberately changed to saké when he realized his health was failing.

As I have mentioned, he mainly drank "one-cups"—a one-cup being a single sealed glass of saké or shōchū. I once asked him why he always bought booze in small quantities. He could get more alcohol for his cash if he bought an *isshōbin*—a big 1.8 liter bottle. But he explained: "If I buy a big bottle, I drink a big bottle." Forcing himself to make frequent trips to the vending machine was a way of controlling a habit which, once the glass was in his hand, became uncontrollable.

One slightly ironic consequence of being on welfare and denied alcohol is that for the first time in his life, Kimitsu has plenty of money. Every month the livelihood protection program pays him about 80,000 yen, on top of his rent, and even after the cost of his delivered meals is deducted, there is well over 50,000 yen left. Since he buys nothing but cigarettes, the occasional snack and sometimes a copy of *Shūkan Bunshun* (his favored conservative weekly magazine), he has a net surplus every month, which is slowly accumulating in his brown envelope at the San'ei Kaikan Helper Station. The helper team has puzzled over this problem of Kimitsu's lack of desire for commodities and even consulted me on how Kimitsu's spare cash might best be used to benefit him. I pointed out Kimitsu's love of jazz music and a small CD player was bought for him, along with a few CDs of jazz classics and oldies. He rarely listens to them.

Being forced off alcohol dramatically improved Kimitsu's health. From being barely able to walk, he became quite sprightly. I recall the day in the fall of 2013 when I took him to the restaurant with the students. Despite his limp, he walked along the street so fast that I had to ask him to wait while the dawdling students caught up. He always had his eye trained straight ahead, and was oblivious to those around him. I worried about him crossing the road—he tended to assume the cars would stop for him.

Though he is one among six thousand in Kotobuki, Kimitsu has quite a few well-wishers. I remember taking him out to the local park on January 3rd, 2013, to see how the Ettō, or Winter Survival Campaign, was going. This is an annual event in Kotobuki, where the day laborer union and others conduct massive food handouts and organize festive New Year events such as rice-cake pounding and karaoke contests, for men who generally cannot go back to their familial homes like many people do at this time of year. We reached the park, with the blue tents of the Ettō headquarters and the medical team, and Kimitsu was recognized by several volunteer medics. They knew he'd been running a fever just the day before, and hurried him into one of the tents to get warm and have his temperature taken. They were heartily relieved to find it had come back almost to normal. It was a moving moment, when I realized that it was not just me who cared for Kimitsu Nishikawa.

Thanks to Dr. Tsuchiya's siege, Kimitsu has lived to celebrate his 74th birthday, and is able to read this book of ours. In 2012, I finally found a publisher for the Japanese edition. It is a tiny one-man publisher in Kyoto called Kyōtotto Press. The owner, Kyōhei Ogawa, took the job very seriously. He even visited Yamaga and took some photos to use in the book. It came out late in 2013, in a cheap paperback edition with plenty of Kimitsu's illustrations.[3]

Figure 4.1. Inside the medical care tent at the Kotobuki Winter Survival Campaign. The author and Kimitsu Nishikawa are sitting on the left.

On November 10, 2013, I took six copies of the book to Kimitsu's room and he signed them. It was supposed to be a moment of celebration—our long collaboration had finally produced a concrete outcome. The old Kimitsu would surely have been delighted, but dementia had taken its toll and he did not seem particularly happy—to be honest, in fact, he hardly showed any expression at all. But I know it did mean something to him, because of the intense care he took over signing the books. It took him about an hour to sign the six copies for friends who had helped me put the book out. He moved the pen agonizingly slowly, drawing elaborate sketches and writing mystifying notes, in English that was on the borderline of being incomprehensible. For his guru, Prof. Shin'ichi Nakazawa, he drew a picture of an elegant blonde lady with a pearl necklace, blowing the guru a kiss along with a baffling jumble of characters. The one for publisher Kyōhei Ogawa had a picture of a man, perhaps a self-portrait, though apparently in Nazi uniform, and said "I MISS YAMAGA. I'LL TRY TRIP AGAIN SOON." Another, for Oxford University Professor Arthur Stockwin, was the only one with a legible version of his name, and it said "NEXT TIME DON'T MISS GETTING SUITABLE TIME" (to meet up again). For Norikazu Todoroki, he wrote the single word "ADVANCE." I think he meant it was an advance copy of the book.

Some of Kimitsu's book inscriptions were more ominous. For Yoshinari Morita, a young anthropologist who also helped check the text, he wrote, I think, "V. SCARY GUILT MEN. NEXT DECADE IT IS 11 CENTURY." (he probably meant twenty-first century, and had forgotten that the century had already started.) "ALSO DEAD MANY PEOPLE." For young Jun'ichi Machida, who had helped check the Japanese for style, he took a red pen and drew a maniacally grinning man holding a bag marked "bomb." The picture was captioned "AT LAST, AT LAST, MONSTER HERO. LOOK." I gave him a black pen and asked him to sign the book with his name. He would not sign it, though. Instead he wrote "Blast, bomb, blast, countdown."

But that was a bad day. Since then I have visited many more times, and he has signed many copies of the book, in his slightly wobbly but elegant handwriting. But since that first day, he hasn't drawn any more pictures or written any more enigmatic messages. And he always signs in Japanese, writing the characters in a slightly unorthodox stroke order.

One result of my twenty-two year association with Kimitsu is that I have reassessed the Japanese social welfare system. Keeping an old man in a three-mat room in a notorious slum district might seem strange, but I always remember what Kimitsu said about Kotobuki, in his distinctive English: "This is my right place." It is where he feels most at home. The care team has done its level best to strike a working compromise between what Kimitsu wants, and what is good for him. For example, they do allow him to buy tobacco, as some compensation for the zero tolerance of alcohol. I cannot argue with that on health grounds, though I pray he will not set the whole doya on fire with a carelessly discarded butt. There are many cigarette burns on the tatami mats. At least his room has a smoke alarm—another thing doya rooms never had in the old days.

As I mentioned, it was always a dream of Kimitsu's and mine to go down to Yamaga and hand a signed copy of our book to his older sister, living there in retirement after a long career as headmistress of a kindergarten. She thought Kimitsu was just a drunken loser, but imagine her surprise when he showed up with a foreign professor and a newly printed book all about him! These initial thoughts of a surprise visit gave way to a more practical idea of getting in touch with her beforehand.

Despite his visits, Kimitsu had no record of her address or phone number. I visited the ward welfare office, and had a talk with Masuko-san, the young man in charge of Kimitsu's livelihood protection records. He had the sister's telephone number. He called it, spoke to her, and got permission to tell me the number.

"What did she say when you told her about this foreign professor who's writing a book about her brother?"

"The first thing she asked was: 'Is his real name going to appear in the book?'"

Of course. To a retired kindergarten teacher, news of my Kimitsu book would not necessarily be welcome. On the contrary, the prospect of the family's reputation being blackened by the appearance of a book about her dissolute brother would be a major concern.

Still, this was a powerful moment for me. Not only was it my first chance to contact Kimitsu's family. It was my first chance to contact a family member of any of the men I had met while studying day laborers in Kotobuki and other doya-gai. Most of the men were completely separated from their natal families, and from their marital families where such existed. Day laborers were little isolated particles, like Kimitsu's diagram of Heisenberg's Uncertainty Principle. In a sense they were easy subjects for fieldwork, since there were no complicated family relationships to be negotiated. Yet now I was going to speak with someone on the other side of the great barrier that separated day laborers from family life. I phoned her on May 31, 2013.

Masuko-san had told her a bit about me, so she was expecting my call. She told me that her son, who still lived with her, had looked me up on the internet and they had even found a photo of me. On the whole she seemed quite pleased and interested to be having the conversation. I introduced myself and told her how indebted I was to her brother Norimitsu for all his help with my research. Like everybody except me, she knew Kimitsu only by his birth-name of Norimitsu.

"You have to understand, I heard nothing from Norimitsu for decades. I really only knew him up to his high-school years. Five or six years ago, he suddenly showed up in Yamaga. He was drunk. It was clear he'd become an alcoholic. He had a one-cup in his hand. Booze was all he wanted. I prepared meals for him, but morning, noon and night, all he wanted was booze. He was always drunk, always unsteady on his feet. He wasn't the Norimitsu I knew.

"But I felt sorry for him, and I gave him 50,000 yen. Now I think that was a mistake. My brother in Osaka told me off—he'll only spend it on booze, he said. He was probably right. After he came once, he came again. I suppose he came four or five times. Maybe he got it into his head that I was a soft touch—although after that first time I never gave him more than 10,000 yen. It would always be late at night when he came, after 11pm. I'd be tucked up in bed, going to sleep, and there'd be this violent banging on the door—and it was him. It was always a shock when it happened—and it disturbed the neighborhood. Everybody wondered what the fuss was all about. So, to be perfectly honest—I didn't like it. Of course, deep down I was relieved to see my brother again, after all those decades, but for the most part it was a big inconvenience.

"To tell you the truth, last year I received a letter from the welfare office, from Masuko-san's predecessor. He told me that Norimitsu had been diagnosed with liver cancer and was very poorly. He'd been saying that before he died, he wanted to go back to Yamaga one more time. He might have to go in a wheelchair. The care-worker said they would take him to the airport in Tokyo and put him on a plane, and wanted to know if I could somehow arrange to meet him at Kumamoto airport. Well, you know my husband is long dead and I have quite a few health problems of my own. I just live here with my son. I really could not see how I was going to look after him in that sort of condition, even just for a couple of days. So I'm sorry to say that I wrote back at great length, saying that I really couldn't do it. I felt so heavy-hearted as I wrote that letter, but what else could I do? It's been preying on my mind ever since."

I told her I completely understood her feelings and did not hold it against her that she had refused to let Norimitsu visit. I added that if we were to arrange a visit now, I would go with him, and probably my wife would come along too, and we would look after him so that it would not be any trouble for her. She did not immediately respond to that suggestion, but did thank me from the bottom of her heart for befriending Norimitsu. Through his long and lonely years of life in a doya room, it must have been a great relief to have someone like me visiting occasionally. Yesterday she'd been talking about it on the phone with the youngest brother in Osaka and they had agreed that they really should thank me for all I had done for him.

"Hontō-ni, sensei no osewa ni natte orimasu."

"We are truly indebted to you, professor."

I told her about Norimitsu's surprising range of knowledge about world affairs, and especially British politics. She replied that Norimitsu often used to be top of the class for social studies when they were at junior high school together. On home visits the social studies teacher had praised his work to their parents. And she was willing to admit that he was an entertaining conversationalist, with his glass of saké in his hand, and she had enjoyed trying to keep up with him when he was in full flow.

"But you know, on his way back to Yokohama after one of those long trips to Yamaga, he had an accident in Hiroshima. He was hit by a train—he could easily have been killed."

Now that she mentioned it, I recalled the incident. He had told he had collapsed on the platform, with his hand over the edge, as a train came in. He pulled back his hand just in time. He smashed the tip of one finger—a fraction of a second slower, and he could have lost a hand, or worse.

"And then the very last time he came to Yamaga, the first I knew of it was when I got a phone call from the hospital. He had collapsed in the street and been taken there by ambulance. That's what drink has done for him, I'm afraid. They got my name from him and called me. I went straight to the hospital. He wasn't in such bad condition, so I took him home in a taxi. Then when I felt he was ready to go home I put him in a taxi all the way to Kumamoto station.[4] I immediately telephoned the welfare office in Yokohama to get them to check for his arrival, and to tell them to try and stop him making any more trips to Kumamoto. It's just so dangerous, you see. He was limping on that final visit, and he had a bandaged finger."

I mentioned Norimitsu's drawings. She said that he had always been keen on drawing—from the age of three or four, he'd be drawing pictures of fighter planes, and foreign soldiers. He drew those pictures all over his exercise books and even on his textbooks. I realized that the style of Kimitsu's German and American soldiers had been honed over close to seventy years.

I asked Kimitsu's older sister about the home film-viewing sessions that Norimitsu often mentioned. She clearly remembered them.

"Our father was a real culture fan. He was very artistic and drew lovely pictures, he went to art shows, and he used to write stories and essays for the in-house magazine at the bank where he worked. He had a passion for music, too. We had a gramophone, at a time when it was still quite a luxury item, and he was an avid record-collector. We grew up surrounded by music. And he loved film. He had a camera as well as a 9.5mm projector.[5] He used to write his own scripts and then film them. He used us children as models. I myself appeared in several films that he made. Our mother was a model for him too, and our youngest brother, though I'm not sure about Norimitsu. I must have been just three or four years old when I started being in his films. He wrote really interesting scripts, you know!

"I was working at the kindergarten, and one time our father came and made a film about a day at a kindergarten. It won a prize in a local contest. When I got married, he made a film of my wedding day. He filmed me having my hair and makeup done, wearing my wedding dress—that won an amateur film prize too.

"Our father died young—he was only 63. He dreamed of making a voyage round the world. I thought that when I was properly employed and earning a salary, maybe I could make enough money to pay for his world cruise—but it was not to be, sadly."

I tried to get back to the subject of Kimitsu.

"How much do you know of Norimitsu's life in the fifty years since he left high school?"

"I knew he was in the SDF. And I knew he was thrown out of the SDF for his drunkenness. I heard from my mother about his visit to Kumamoto University Hospital when dad was in there dying of cancer. It was terrible. He was already drunk when he arrived, and he was wandering around the hospital wards, shouting things nobody could understand—in English. Yes, he was talking all in English, that's what mother said. After that he abandoned us and I don't know anything about the next forty years."

"A long time after father died, mother was in touch with him for a while. She tried to send him a letter now and again, and sometimes a little present. But he said that at the kind of place he was living, the presents wouldn't get through properly so she should stop sending them. So we kind of gave up on him. There was no more contact at all until our other brother was killed in that traffic accident. He was hit by a taxi, so we got money from the insurance company. But the paperwork needed everybody to put their personal seal on it, so my other brother made inquiries to see if Norimitsu was still alive, and finally traced him to Kotobuki. That was how contact was re-established. We didn't know where he was when mother died, and had no way of letting him know. To be honest, we thought he'd probably died in the gutter somewhere—that seemed likely to be his fate."

Finally, I raised the subject of the book. I knew it was a difficult topic. Already the image of her delighted face as Kimitsu and I handed over the book was wavering. I realized that I was not sure whether or not she knew about the assault case and two-and-a-half year jail sentence, or the encounters with prostitutes in Susukino. Still, I hesitantly asked her if she might be willing to have a look at the manuscript and give me her thoughts. She too was hesitant.

"You have to remember, this is the first I've heard about all the books and intellectualizing. I thought he was just a hopeless alcoholic. So frankly, I didn't feel very good about it when I heard about the book. I'm really amazed by what you've been telling me."

"Do you want to read the manuscript? I've tried to present a full picture of Norimitsu. There'll be places that make you feel ashamed of him, but others where you'll feel proud of him."

A long, long pause.

"I want to read it, and I don't want to read it. On the whole I think it might be better if I don't read it. If I read it, I might not want you to publish it."

In the end, Kimitsu's sister preferred not to see the book and asked me not to send her the manuscript. I did get in touch with her again one more time, to ask her about the 9.5mm films. She appears to be sitting on a treasure trove of antique home movies, and I found a professor of film studies who was willing to undertake the otherwise very expensive work of transferring them to DVD for free if he could use the DVDs for research purposes. For a moment the dream of handing the book to Kimitsu's sister was replaced by one of showing Kimitsu his childhood on a TV screen—but in the end Kimitsu's sister, after consulting with her brother in Osaka, decided she didn't want to do that either.

In the spring of 2014 I organized a series of events for Kimitsu to promote our book. Three times I took him on day trips to Tokyo. We addressed two study groups—the Marunouchi Square seminar run by lawyer Kanji Ishizumi and the Minorities seminar run by Prof. Yasunori Fukuoka (emeritus) of Saitama University. We also visited Prof. Naofumi Nakamura of the Institute of Social Science at University of Tokyo, who by a tremendous coincidence hails from Yamaga. The two men enjoyed reminiscing about the town.

Then on April 12, 2014, I organized a 74th birthday party for Kimitsu, at a restaurant near Kotobuki. Dr. Tsuchiya came along, as did my wife and several activists from the day laborer union. Dr. Tsuchiya and I drank soft drinks out of solidarity for Kimitsu. She had assembled a paper bag full of books donated by doctors and healthcare workers at the Kotobuki clinic. They were of the kind Kimitsu used to enjoy reading—about art, anarchism and other weighty topics.

Kimitsu's face was largely immobile, but he did manage a smile when we sang Happy Birthday.

Afterwards we took Kimitsu back to his room. It was only a five-minute walk, but he had to stop twice for a breather.

Twice in the following months I accompanied Kimitsu to the Yokohama City University Medical Center in Urafune-chō to sit in on consultations about his liver cancer. This was at the request of Dr. Tsuchiya, for Kimitsu has no relatives in town to help him think about serious medical issues. As we have seen, his older sister and younger brother both know where he is, but they do not want to get involved. To this day, he is an embarrassment to the family.

A CT-scan was conducted in June 2014, which showed that the cancerous growths in Kimitsu's liver had started to spread. The doctor—speaking very bluntly considering the reputation of the Japanese medical reputation for concealing unpleasant truths from patients—outlined two scenarios. Kimitsu could undergo a series of surgical procedures like the ones he'd had before, inserting a catheter into his liver to drip medicine onto the affected area. Each time it was done he would have to spend a week or so in hospital. It would be quite painful and debilitating, but it might enable him to live another two or three years. Alternatively, the growths could be left untreated. Kimitsu would live in relative comfort, but perhaps only for another year or so.

The doctor spoke in such a plain, matter-of-fact way that for a moment it did not feel as though somebody's imminent death was being discussed. Kimitsu's expressionless face revealed nothing of what impression the doctor's words had made. He just sat there on his little round hospital stool and said nothing. I and his care-worker, Jurō Andō, encouraged him to say something. "I think we should do what we can. I'll go for it," he finally said. The doctor told him to have a careful think about it. A couple of weeks later, Dr. Tsuchiya told me that Kimitsu had changed his mind. He had hated the previous surgical procedures, and he did not want to go through them again. He saw no point in enduring more pain to prolong his life, and was resigned to engaging in *shūkatsu*. In Japanese, this word is usually written with the kanji 就活, and it means "employment activities," hence "job-hunting." But Kimitsu was thinking of the ironic alternative writing 終活, meaning "end activities"—i.e., preparation for death.

On August 14, 2014, I went to the Kotobuki summer festival rock concert to sell copies of the Japanese edition of this book. I managed to find Kimitsu at one of the day-care centers he attends, where he was sitting in the improvised smoking corner—a tiny area behind a partition with an open window and a bucket of water. He had a lit cigarette in hand, and was staring at the floor. The care manager allowed me to take him to the festival and for an hour or two he sat with me at a table next to the concert stage, deafened by rock music, which made conversation impossible, while I sold copies of the book to passers-by. We sold thirty-seven. Later I went to see him at his room. He was begging me to give him money so that he could buy a drink. "387 . . . 516 . . . 476 . . . 602 . . . " He was mumbling numbers. I finally figured out that these were examples of sums of cash, in yen, that would be suitable for buying a couple of drinks. I reminded him of his arrangement with Dr. Tsuchiya. "Oh that . . . hahaha . . . she is right, of course. But isn't it interesting and funny . . . normally it's men who make trouble for women, but this time it's the other way round."

To be honest, I did treat him to just one drink. I wonder if Dr. Tsuchiya will forgive me.

That would be a nice note on which to end my narrative, but time always rolls on. The rest of the summer passed by with me in England for several weeks. Then I had to go back to work at the university. Finally, on October 1, 2014, I called up Jurō Andō, head of the helper station looking after Kimitsu at the San'ei Kaikan. His mental condition had noticeably worsened. His episodes of *haikai*—wandering around lost—were increasing. He would more frequently walk into somebody else's room by accident. He had forgotten how to use the elevator and would wobble precariously up and down the staircase instead. He did not know which floor he was living on and had to be guided home by a care worker when found roaming about the building. On one occasion he had been found asleep on the floor in the lobby of the building.

Things like visits to the two day-care centers he patronized, and to Dr. Tsuchiya's clinic, he could no longer do alone. He now had to be accompanied by a care worker. The level of care in his room had also been stepped up. Whereas he used to be visited by a care worker three times a week—on the days when he did not go to a day-care center—now he was being visited every day.

His appetite was variable. After he had left a lot of food for some time, they had reduced the food deliveries to twice a day—morning and evening. This would be supplemented with the occasional bread roll or sandwich which his care worker would buy for him on demand. He had lost a bit of weight.

Kimitsu's days of intense reading were behind him now. The care workers would still buy him a weekly magazine now and again, but he could barely read them with his big metal-rimmed reading glasses from the hundred-yen shop.

His smoking habit was a growing cause for concern. Despite the large bucket of water always by his bedside, he was still in the habit of dropping lighted cigarettes on the floor, and the burn marks on the tatami mats were steadily increasing. A complaint had also been received about his habit of throwing cigarette butts out of the window into the street below—a very traditional doya-gai practice not considered acceptable these days.

The alarmed care workers had reduced his tobacco allowance. Often when I visited Kimitsu I would notice six or seven packs of cigarettes on the shelf in his cupboard—a tolerant view of smoking was a kind of compensation for demanding abstinence from alcohol. Now they had reduced the supply to one or two packs at a time. But Andō-san had noticed that if Kimitsu ran out of cigarettes, he was likely to get nervous and set out on one of his random walks around the building. The care worker would pop out and buy him a packet if he ran out, but these half-hearted measures were no safeguard against fire.

It is sad when an old man loses his faculties and drifts towards death. But how much sadder if he dies in a fire that takes other innocent lives with him. Every night I prayed that Kimitsu would not end his life in a fiery holocaust.

Then, early in November 2014, the manager of Kimitsu's doya reluctantly told his care manager, Mr. Andō, that he wanted Kimitsu to leave. There had been more complaints about his tendency to wander into other people's rooms, help himself to their cigarettes, and go to sleep in their beds. He could no longer use the elevator. He did not know which floor to go to, and Andō-san noticed that when he tried to use it, his finger would miss the buttons, instead pressing the wall next to the button. So he would wander up and down the stairs. He had been found asleep in the stairwell. He had also got lost a few times while wandering around Kotobuki, and on one occasion had been brought back home by the police. He had even tried to get warm by lighting a fire in the metal bucket in his room—rather than switching on the air conditioning.

Altogether, he had become a danger to himself and others.

Dr. Tsuchiya arranged for Kimitsu to check into Kanagawa Hospital, some 15 miles away from Kotobuki, to undergo a period of rest and a more controlled lifestyle. In his last few days at the San'ei Kaikan, he did not make any more trouble for people. Murata-san, one of his long-suffering care workers, observed that he was lying down most of the time and seemed tired. He made no objection when Dr. Tsuchiya told him about the stay in hospital.

On November 14, Kimitsu left Kotobuki in the company of a care worker, heading for hospital, date of return uncertain. As I write, he is in the dementia ward, surrounded by others with similar or worse conditions. His medical care is covered by the welfare system, but there would be a wait of a year or two for a place in a public care home, and a private one would cost a lot of money. So for now he remains in hospital, though not exactly ill, except for his gradually progressing liver cancer, while the care team wonders what to do with him next. In Japan such cases are called *shakaiteki nyūin*—'social hospitalization'—where the primary reason for being in hospital is not medical but social. The patient is in hospital because there is nowhere else to go.

NOTES

1. From Naka ward office figures for 2013 that show 5,242 welfare recipients in a total doya population of 6,322.
2. In 2014, the maximum rent payable for a single person under the livelihood protection system is 53,700 yen a month—about $500 at the prevailing exchange rate. Most of the better doya in Kotobuki charge more than that. The welfare office makes up the difference by treating men like Kimitsu as disabled, in which case the upper limit is 69,800 yen.
3. *Mainichi Ahōdansu: Kotobuki-chō no Hiyatoi Tetsugakusha Nishikawa Kimitsu no Sekai* (Everyday Affordance: The World of Kimitsu Nishikawa, the Day-Laboring Philosopher of Kotobuki-chō). Kyoto: Kyōtotto Press.
4. This would have been an expensive fare—the distance is some 40 kilometers.
5. I later ascertained that she was talking about the 9.5mm Pathé Baby amateur film format, which was quite popular in Japan in the 1930s and 1940s.

Chapter Five

Commentary

It would be irresponsible to end this book without making some attempt to place Kimitsu in his social context in contemporary Japanese society, and to interpret the things Kimitsu said in our many conversations. In this final section I will take on those challenges one after the other.

Several people have asked me whether I view Kimitsu as unique, or as typical of the people in his social class. The answer is both. Clearly his is a unique, distinctive voice. He is incomparably better read than any other day laborer I have met, and his interests range more widely than those of any other day laborer. Yet he is far from being the only philosopher, or social observer, in the yoseba. A good example would be Shiro Oyama,[1] the pseudonym of the narrator of *San'ya Gakeppuchi Nikki* (San'ya: A Diary of Life on the Edge; Hankyū Communication, 2000), a prize-winning book translated into English by Edward Fowler as *A Man With No Talents* (Cornell University Press, 2005). Oyama, who unlike Kimitsu had a university education, is a sharp, mordant observer of life in the doya-gai. The English title is taken from a passage where he says, "I am, in short, a man with no talents who is incapable of relating to women or coping with work" (Oyama 128). Like Kimitsu, he confesses to never having slept with a woman without paying (ibid.). But he casts a bleaker eye on doya-gai society than does Kimitsu. Where Kimitsu will occasionally celebrate a spirit of comradeship among day laborers, Oyama writes, "I have lived a total of fifteen years as a day laborer, yet I have never beheld the kind of lofty or beautiful human spirit that people somehow expect to witness at the bottom of society. . . . I have lost count of the men I have run across who embody a veritable trinity of ignorance, meanness, and arrogance" (Oyama 117). Despite his many admissions of personal weakness, Kimitsu never descends to the loathing and self-loathing of Oyama. His is a more tolerant, balanced perspective.

Other comparative studies may be found in the "Lives" section of *San'ya Blues*, Edward Fowler's book on life in San'ya, the Tokyo doya-gai, and in the short character sketches at the end of each chapter in my own *Men of Uncertainty*. The man with the greatest intellectual aspirations was Sakae (pp. 10–12), an engineer who admired Werner von Braun and was trying to develop an embossing machine in an apartment he rented away from Kotobuki. He had a philosophical bent, too, and dreamed of one day achieving a kind of immortality by embossing a three-dimensional image of his own face onto a stone: "Then I'm going to go to some cliff, and throw the stone out to sea, so that even after millions of years, long after I'm dead, I'll still be there. That's my dream" (Gill, *Men of Uncertainty*: 12).

In December 2008, another distinctive voice emerged from Kotobuki, with the publication in the *Asahi Shinbun* newspaper of a *tanka* (a 31-syllable poem) by a self-styled homeless poet called Kō'ichi Kōda.

Carrying my soft watch, I wait in line two hours for the curry they're handing out.

Over the next nine months he had a series of works selected by the four judges of the newspaper's Monday feature for readers' tanka. He became known as one of the most brilliant amateur poets the newspaper had ever stumbled upon.

I go to sleep clutching a can of hot coffee; awaking, I sip cold coffee.

Seven minutes of ecstasy: soaking my body in a coin shower on a cold day.

They call my kind unfilial, but I have no parents, and have never become a parent; all I do is just stand here.

Kōda became a minor celebrity. It was clear from references in the poems that he was living in or around Kotobuki—there aren't many places with public coin-operated showers—but he refused to supply the newspaper with means of locating him.

Man cannot live on bread alone—yet I live this day on a crust of bread from a hand-out.

Reading an article about a homeless tanka poet as though it had nothing to do with me, I do not shed a tear.

With pain in my chest, I have taken medical welfare and am in a room like a coffin here in the doya-gai.

In September 2009, the last of Kōda's tanka was published in the Asahi and the postcards with his works stopped coming to the newspaper offices. Several people made determined efforts to find him, including Takashi Miyama, a freelance journalist who wrote a book about his search for Kōda, during which he himself lived on the streets of Kotobuki (*Hōmuresu Kajin ga iru Fuyu*; 'The winter when there was a homeless poet'; Bungei Shunju, 2011). In the end Kōda was never identified or interviewed. But he remains as another example of a voice which, like Kimitsu's, is both distinctive and representative of doya-gai life.

Kimitsu's career is also typical enough to afford insight into the lives of men at the bottom end of Japanese society. The 6,000 men who live in Kotobuki share a lifestyle, a look, and certain socioeconomic characteristics. As I showed in *Men of Uncertainty*, the great majority of day laborers in Japan are from rural backgrounds, and it would appear that a surprisingly high proportion—about 40 percent in my sample—are eldest sons.[2] This is the case with Kimitsu. Shame at his inability to fulfill family expectations of the role of the first-born son is a recurrent theme. Admittedly being the son of a banker he does not match the lowly class background of his peers, but the narrative shows how the war cost his father his job and much of his social status, as well as costing Kimitsu the chance to go to college, leaving private study as his only option for intellectual advancement. His stint in the military, and his stint in prison, are also experiences shared by many of the other men in Kotobuki.

Thus his story shows us how post-war Japan has treated a class of men who, for a variety of reasons, were unable to achieve the stereotypical aspirations of a steady job, stable housing, and married life. It is a sometimes brutal story of men used when useful to the construction and longshoring industries, then cast aside when no longer needed. Yet chapter 4 above lends some lighter tones, as we learn how improvements in the administration of social welfare in Japan (and especially Yokohama) have brought an end to the era where retirement, for a day laborer, meant homelessness and death on the street.

At the same time that implementation of welfare systems has been gradually eased in Japan, however, we have also seen a sharp increase in the percentage of the workforce employed in short-term, unstable, and low-wage employment. As the guarantee of stable employment has eroded, we have seen a proliferation of insecure labor arrangements, with a complex vocabulary. In addition to traditional categories such as *pāto* (part-timer, though the worker may in fact be working full-time hours), *keiyaku sha'in* (contract worker), and *shokutaku* (contract specialist), we also have a large population of *arubaitā* (from the German word "arbeiter" or worker; people doing part-time jobs call *arubaito* or *baito* for short). The image of an *arubaitā* is of a young person, typically a high school or college student. When an *arubaitā* is still doing insecure part-time work after leaving education, he or she may well be called a *furītā*, or freeter, which is a contraction of "free arbeiter," an English-German concatenation that stresses the freedom of the arrangement rather than its insecurity.

But there is another, very important kind of insecure labor in Japan—namely, labor that is mediated through a dispatch agency, whereby the employer and the workplace are two separate entities. This pattern of employment is spreading rapidly in Japan, and elsewhere in East Asia, notably China. The worker is paid by the dispatch agency, which bills the end employer for the worker's services, typically adding a commission of 30 percent or more as its fee for supplying the worker. Employers are willing to pay this substantial premium because they are absolved from any responsibility for the worker's continued employment and can use them or get rid of them at will. They simply inform the dispatch agency that the worker's services will no longer be required from the following month, and the agency regretfully passes on the bad news. This ability to avoid responsibility helps to explain the prevalence of dispatch agencies, sub-contractors and other indirect forms of employment in hazardous forms of employment such as the nuclear power industry. Since the Fukushima nuclear disaster of March 2011, it has emerged that the operator of the Fukushima No. 1 nuclear power plant, Tokyo Electric Power, did not even know the names of some of the personnel working at the plant. Such is the distancing effect of indirect employment.

When I first arrived in Japan, in 1983, worker dispatch agencies (*jinzai haken gyōsha*) were illegal. Having been effectively banned under the Labor Stabilization Law just after World War II, they were partially legalized in 1966 and then greatly deregulated by the Nakasone government in 1986, under the 1985 Labor Dispatch Law (*Rōdō Haken-hō*). Various industrial sectors were excluded from the deregulation, but the last of these restrictions was lifted in 2003. Over the last thirty years, labor dispatch companies such as Recruit, Pasona, Tempstaff and Fullcast have developed to the point where they constitute a major branch of the labor market. The world of dispatch workers has its own hierarchy, including the relatively elite *jōyō haken* (regular dispatched worker, who collects a salary from the dispatch agency even when they do not have a position for him at an end employer; relatively few in number, mostly male and with some kind of technical specialization); the more insecure *tōroku haken* (registered dispatch worker, who registers for work with an agency but only gets a salary when working for an end employer; they are far more numerous and overwhelmingly female); *hiyatoi haken rōdōsha* (dispatched worker employed on a daily basis); and *supotto haken rōdōsha* (ad hoc dispatched worker). People in these last two, mutually overlapping categories are also called "one call workers" (*wan kōru wākā*) because they can be called up and offered employment for the day just by a simple call to their mobile telephone. In fact it is usually an electronic message rather than a traditional phone call: the dispatch agencies maintain sites where a worker can register which days they are available, which hours they can work, and what kinds of work they are willing to do. The agency's computer will then attempt to match them with employers who require workers. Viewed positively, it is a sophisticated system for facilitating flexible working arrangements; but there is no guarantee that a call will come on any given day, and workers unwilling to register for anti-social hours and hard physical labor may find it hard to get placements.

There are some important differences between these employment practices and the kind of day labor practiced by Kimitsu and the other men of the yoseba/doya-gai. Perhaps the most important one, which I discussed in the epilogue to *Men of Uncertainty* (pp. 191–198),[3] is the decline of solidarity among insecurely employed workers. The word "yoseba" literally means "a place to gather people" and it is a concrete location which brings together workers who are looking for casual employment. In the yoseba they may engage in fierce competition for work, but there is at least the possibility of solidarity: workers are in a shared situation and may help each other out when injustices occur. Kimitsu likes to emphasize this side of life in Kotobuki, as do the men of the Kotobuki Day Laborer Union (*Kotobuki-chō Hiyatoi Rōdōsha Kumiai*, or *Junichirō* for short; see p. 25 above). In contrast, as we have just seen, Oyama, writing about San'ya, does not believe there is much solidarity or kindred spirit among day laborers. But one thing is undeniably true: the yoseba brings workers together, whether it be to help each other or spite each other. As I wrote: "Whether you go there to shop for disposable labor, to earn a crust, or to instill political awareness, there is a shared interest in the simple act of coming together which may help to account for the historical continuity of the institution. From the workers' point of view, it is both exploitative and functional. Being there is stigmatized; not being there would arguably be worse. The yoseba gives day laborers a place to exchange information on employment conditions and a web of personal connections which help to dispel anomie and can be a valuable safety net in times of trouble."[4]

Now contrast that with the one-call worker. His connection with the worksite is mediated through cyberspace. He looks for job offers on his mobile phone and he may never see another worker in a similar situation except at the worksite. He is spared the trouble of going to a location in the city different from the location where he will work—but he is also deprived of the company of his fellow workers. So much depends on a single item of hardware: the mobile telephone. Its arrival has spelled the end for traditional day-laboring arrangements. Nowadays the use of the yoseba as a labor market is largely limited to people who cannot afford to have a mobile telephone—which marks them out as being at a particularly low level of the proletariat. But for people who do own a mobile phone and know how to use it, there is at least the possibility of a new kind of solidarity. If one builds up contacts and uses the internet skillfully, it is possible to inform a lot of people very quickly if some employment abuse occurs.

There have been several attempts to make use of the mobile phone as an organizing tool by unions that have sought to organize dispatch workers. One fairly well-known example is the Haken Union (HU),[5] which was founded in 2005 and has sought to combat abusive practices in the labor dispatch industry. Their slogans, "One for all, all for one," "United we stand, divided we fall," and "Where there is unity, there is victory," indicate a conscious attempt to take up the baton of left-wing activism long associated with the day laborer union movement centered on the yoseba. The union had a notable success in 2007, when it accused a large labor dispatch agency, Goodwill, of unjustly making deductions from pay in the name of "data-processing fees" (*dētā sōbi-hi*) and ultimately managed to force the company to put an end to the practice. Goodwill became embroiled in several other scandals involving illegal exploitation of workers and was finally forced into liquidation at the end of 2009.[6]

But the occasional victory like this cannot distract from the fact that the position of dispatch workers vis-à-vis their employers is incomparably weaker than that of their directly-employed co-workers. When regular salaries are converted into hourly rates, dispatch workers earn on the average less than half the wages of regular employees,[7] who usually get two or three bonuses a year, their travel expenses paid, and a range of fringe benefits in addition to their basic wage. Crucially, wages for regular workers go up steadily with age, whereas those for dispatch workers remain almost unchanged throughout the working career. A report by Haken Rōdō Nettowāku (Dispatch Labor Network) finds that wages for the two types of employee are roughly the same at age 20, but regular workers in their 40s and 50s earn more than twice as much as dispatch workers the same age.[8] They can be dismissed at will with a month's notice, and of course the "one call workers" can be used and discarded just like a traditional day laborer at the drop of a hat. This was brutally demonstrated after the 2008 Lehmann Shock: as recession spread to Japan, many companies laid off their dispatched personnel, and *haken-gire* (cutting dispatch workers) became a notorious economic phenomenon. Around the same time, *waakingu pua* (working poor) became a popular topic in news and current affairs—as it still is today, along with *buraku kigyō* (black enterprises), the shady companies that employ people on particularly low wages and without job security.

What this all means is that where once men like Kimitsu were truly marginalized outliers, they are now part of a much broader spectrum of people living without the comforting guarantees of the salaryman lifestyle. True, the number of people working out of the yoseba has greatly declined, and nowadays there are so few jobs available at the day laboring employment exchange that it has more or less ceased to function. Government statistics for 2013 show that there are just 20,000 people still carrying the white handbook (*shiro techō*; officially "day laborer unemployment insurance handbook" or *hiyatoi shitsugyō hoken techō*) that allows entitlement to day-laborer unemployment insurance under the system created in 1953.[9] This was an idealistic post-war attempt to bring some kind of stability to people hired on a daily basis, and to this day the system is largely unchanged: by sticking revenue stamps in the book for each day employed, one acquires the right to a daily payment of 7,500 yen per day not employed in the month following a two-month period with at least 26 days worked.

Kimitsu discusses this system on pages 6 and 8 above. Though he is correct in his analysis that the system is designed to help day laborers who can get fairly regular employment and discards those who cannot, it is still a rare example of an attempt to unite two very disparate concepts, of casual labor and unemployment insurance. The program is heavily subsidized by the government—the daily revenue stamp costs just 176 yen, theoretically paid for 50–50 by employer and worker, which is a tiny fraction of the 7,500 yen benefit that can be paid out on roughly the same number of days that the premium is paid.[10]

In contrast with the 20,000 registered day laborers, the government statistics for households by form of employment show 326,000 households dependent on day labor, or 0.7 percent of the total, as of 2012. A further 2,203,000, or 4.6 percent of the total, were dependent on short-term (*rinji*) employment. In these statistics, "day labor" includes people working on contracts of less than one month, and "short-term" includes people working on contracts of one month to one year. But many other households are subsumed in the amorphous category of "self-employed" (5,440,000 or 11.3%) and "other" (13,837,000 or 28.7%). Only 25,462,000 or 52.9 percent of households were classified as depending on regular (*jōyō*) employment.[11] The big picture that emerges from these statistics is a rather literal one of two nations—just over half the households in Japan living on some kind of regular employment, just under half falling into various irregular categories. So while the traditional style of day labor practiced by Kimitsu is now a very minor element in the Japanese labor market, more broadly defined irregular labor is close to accounting for half the working population. Though some academics have hailed the spread of "atypical" working arrangements as adding flexibility to the labor market,[12] the great majority see the erosion of job security as a major problem afflicting the Japanese economy today.

Most people in irregular employment do not have an effective form of unemployment insurance—not even the ad-hoc style of insurance of the day laborer's white handbook. This means that when they fall out of employment, they must rely on savings, family support networks, or on Japan's social welfare system of last resort—livelihood protection, or *seikatsu hogo*. This is the system that has saved Kimitsu from destitution. By global standards, it is a generous system. Livelihood protection pays roughly 80,000 yen ($800) a month, plus one's rent up to a maximum of about 50,000 yen ($500), along with free medical and dental care. The story of Kimitsu's old age reminds us that despite much talk of a rightward shift in Japanese politics in recent years, this is a state that still has a relatively humane welfare system. To put it in perspective, consider the nearest equivalent to livelihood protection in the United States—General Relief (also called General Assistance in some states). In the supposedly generous state of California, GR pays $221 a month. Supplemental Security Income (SSI) pays $877.40 a month, but only to people over 65 or with a disability.

There are those who think that livelihood protection is *too* generous. The minimum wage in Yokohama as of October 2014 is 887 yen per hour. Assuming a 40-hour working week, that works out at around 150,000 yen a month, which is only slightly above the livelihood protection level. People working less than 40 hours a week can easily end up earning less than livelihood protection. Feelings are especially strong regarding places like Kotobuki, where there are plenty of bars and illegal-but-tolerated gambling houses, where at least some of the livelihood protection money is spent. To some cynical observers, the system appears to transfer money from the taxpayer to the yakuza gangsters who run many of those establishments, with only a brief stay in the pocket of the retired day laborer who is supposed to be having his livelihood protected. Livelihood protection payments come in during the first week in the month, and there is no mistaking the festive atmosphere in that first week around the bars and gambling houses in Kotobuki, nor the quietness of the final week of the month. The Kotobuki day laborer union still hands out hot meals every Friday afternoon, and there are always several hundred men patiently waiting in line. Some of them no doubt are receiving livelihood protection and stretching their budgets for alcohol and gambling by getting a free meal. Similarly, Christian groups sometimes visit Kotobuki and hand out food to those who are willing to sit through a sermon and sing some hymns (figure 5.1). This practice is known locally as "*amen de ramen*"—saying "amen" in order to get a bowl of ramen noodles. The spread of welfare to the population of Kotobuki has not apparently reduced demand for these charitable hand-outs.

Figure 5.1. A line of men getting free noodles at a missionary prayer meeting in Kotobuki.

The livelihood protection system is based on the right of the individual to decide how to spend the money received, although special arrangements can be made with the agreement of the individual, as in the case of Kimitsu's cash-free lifestyle. Still, most of the welfare-recipients in Kotobuki receive 130–140,000 yen on or just after the first of the month, out of which they must typically pay 66,000–68,200 yen to the doya landlord for rent at 2,200 yen a night—the upper limit set by the city authorities. The rest they are free to use sensibly or foolishly as they see fit.

Be that as it may, one thing that can be stated with some certainty is that the more liberal approach to accepting welfare applications in recent years has brought down the number of homeless people in Japan. The annual national count held every January has shown a steady decline from the 25,292 recorded in 2003, and reached a low of 7,508 in 2014, consisting of 6,929 men, 266 women and 313 "gender unclear."[13] There are a few criticisms to be made of the count: there are likely to be fewer people sleeping outdoors in the winter than the summer, for example, and the timing of the count, usually in the evening, is likely to miss some people who have not yet bedded down for the night; also the count tends to focus on areas where relatively many homeless people are known to sleep, thereby overlooking those who stay away from the crowd. Sometimes what are really counted are homeless dwellings—shacks and tents—which helps to account for the "gender unclear" category. Also, the count focuses narrowly on street homeless, what are called "rough sleepers" in the UK, and there is no attempt made to count other populations viewed as homeless in many countries, such as those living in shelters, or unstable temporary accommodation such as a doya room.

Despite these reservations, it does seem undeniable that there has been a downward trend in street homelessness in Japan. Certainly the figures compare well with most other industrialized nations, and especially well with the USA, where attempts to estimate the national homeless population—a daunting task—have in recent years fallen in the area of 600–700,000 including both street homeless and sheltered homeless. A recent report by the National Alliance to End Homelessness counted 215,344 people living "on the streets or other places not meant for human habitation" on a single night in January 2013, with a further 394,698 people sleeping in shelters for a total homeless population of 610,042.[14] Taking the difference in population into account, and counting only narrowly defined street homeless, the US homeless rate is about 11 times higher than Japan's. The big gap in basic welfare provision helps explain why Japan has a relatively low rate of homelessness compared to the United States—livelihood protection is a far more effective safety net than the patchwork of programs in the US, varying from state to state, and including General Relief/General Assistance, Supplemental Security Income, food stamps, Medicaid, Medicare, etc.[15]

If the livelihood protection system is a major factor in Japan's relatively low rate of homelessness, then changes in the principles used in applying it are an important element in the decline in Japan's homeless population over the last decade or so. As I mentioned in the introduction, Japanese welfare authorities used to refuse applications from anyone using a doya room as an address, since the flophouses are supposed to be temporary lodging places rather than permanent residences. But since the successful campaign by the day laborer union and others in the Kotobuki Association for Winning the Right to Live (see p. 25 above), Yokohama has led the way in introducing a more realistic and humane policy, and nowadays men no longer able to make a living as day laborers are not generally abandoned by the state—at least not if they are over the age of 60. As Kimitsu would put it, the "affordance" of the city of Yokohama has loosened and allowed a more dignified old age to the men of Kotobuki.

Nowadays it is relatively straightforward to apply for livelihood protection in Kotobuki. You go to the Naka-ward welfare office, tell the officials that you have no means of supporting yourself, and fill in the application form. The box where you write your address can be left blank. The welfare official will give you 3,000 yen, which is enough to pay for one night in a doya and buy some very basic food. The next day, you go back to the welfare office and complete the application, using the address of the doya where you spent the night. The welfare office investigates your application for about two weeks, during which the nightly rent on the doya room piles up, to be paid in arrears when the application is accepted. The investigation is not very thorough. It entails checking your credit history and writing to your next of kin to ask if they are willing and able to support you. Sometimes this letter receives a reply stating that the relative is financially constrained himself and unable to support the applicant; sometimes there is no reply at all. In such cases the welfare officials usually conclude that the applicant does indeed have no means of support, and they approve the application. During the two weeks of the investigation, the applicant has to make daily visits to the welfare office where he is paid 1,000 yen to buy food for the day. Thus he is able to eke out a minimal living until the application is approved.

It is no surprise that one outcome of the growth in insecure labor has been a big increase in people living on livelihood protection. The 5,000 people in Kotobuki who use the system are but the tip of a large iceberg. From a low of 882,000 in 1995 (monthly mean), the number of recipients of livelihood protection in the whole of Japan has risen every year, to reach 2,158,840 in June 2014. Almost every month the record is broken. The dire state of public finance in Japan, where the national debt is reckoned to be about 1,000 trillion yen, or 2.5 times annual GDP, means that the beneficence afforded to Kimitsu and his like may not last indefinitely. In the summer of 2013 the Abe administration instituted a series of cuts to livelihood protection designed to reduce payments incrementally by about 10 percent. This is one small part of a mighty struggle to cope with the ballooning national debt.

The situation is no less dire at the local level—Kanagawa prefecture, of which Yokohama is the prefectural capital, has generated a deficit every year since 1991 and has accumulated 1.895 trillion yen of debt in that period.[16] Essentially the ballooning national and local deficits, and the steady rise in people needing welfare—of which livelihood protection is just one part—are a pair of trains, on collision course.

A look at Japan's Gini coefficient gives an idea of the problem. Gini is a well-known way of measuring wealth inequality. It varies between 0 and 1, with a score close to zero indicating a high degree of equality and a score close to one indicating a high degree of inequality. Statistics cover the Gini coefficient before tax and social spending, and after. In 1981 Japan had a relatively low pre-tax/spending Gini coefficient of 0.330, but that had reached 0.421 by 1990, at the end of the bubbly 1980s. By 2002 it was 0.498 and by 2011, a shocking 0.554. However, redistribution by taxes and social spending kept the adjusted Gini at about 0.38 from 1999 to 2011. In 1999, tax/spend redistribution brought the Gini down by 19.2 percent. In 2011, tax/spend redistribution brought the Gini down by 31.5 percent.[17] In other words, government is having to work harder and harder through the welfare system to offset the steady widening of inequality in Japanese society. A lot of the money used to do that has been borrowed; hence the spiraling national debt. Quite soon, the situation will no longer be sustainable.

The truth is that Kimitsu's state-supported old age is one tiny element in a structural malaise in which the falling birthrate and aging population steadily reduce the number of people contributing to public finances and increase the number of people needing help from them. The increasing number of people with low and insecure incomes sits on the back of that structural malaise. Of course the two problems feed into each other, since people with low and insecure incomes cannot generally contemplate getting married and starting a family. I have the strong feeling that Kimitsu was very lucky in the timing of his day-laboring career and "retirement" to livelihood protection.

Now I will attempt a closer analysis of Kimitsu's narrative.

In a sense his whole life has been a slowly fading echo of war. Though he was only five years old when World War II ended, it dominates his conversation and his thought. Somehow the dates do not quite work. Since he was born in April 1940, and the war ended in August 1945, the long walks in the mountains with his father, the reading of propaganda magazines, the viewing of wartime newsreels, and the treasured times with his grandfather, must all have happened before his sixth birthday. He would have been not quite two years old when General Yamashita took Singapore. I several times challenged Kimitsu about this, but he always insisted that these were vivid memories from the earliest phase of his life. Either Kimitsu was a very precocious child, or his memory has transposed later experiences back to the war years.

A revealing moment in the narrative comes when Kimitsu admits that as a five-year-old boy he could not tell the difference between the big blond German soldiers he saw on his father's newsreel and the big blond American soldiers who arrived in Kumamoto under the postwar occupation (p. 39). To him it seemed that the same supermen had conquered first Europe and now Japan. His deeply ingrained habit of drawing all sorts of characters so that they look like stereotypical Aryan soldiers, with blond wavy hair, prominent noses and high foreheads, probably stems from this powerful childhood impression. If pressed, he will reluctantly admit that there were soldiers with dark hair or small stature, and indeed negroes, in the US occupying forces. Most of the time, however, that variety is edited out.

There are two great axes to the way people think about soldiers and war: in terms of good and evil, and in terms of strong and weak. Nowadays there is a general consensus that the Nazi project was evil. In that case the Americans who fought the Nazis would presumably be good. But to a Japanese schoolboy, that American goodness was deeply compromised. Until August 15, 1945, they had been an implacable foe, depicted with their British allies as *Bei-ei kichiku* (American and British devils). They had dropped atomic bombs on Hiroshima and Nagasaki and destroyed many other Japanese cities with incendiaries. Nearer home, they had also killed 500 people in a bombing raid on Kimitsu's birthplace, Kumamoto city. To accept such people as heroes of freedom and democracy would be a lot to ask of a small Japanese boy.

The other axis, of strength and weakness, was altogether easier for the young Kimitsu to understand. Blond supermen were powerful; he and his fellow Japanese were weak—full stop.

Japanese ambiguity about the war in the Pacific is a political issue to this day. Most will agree that it was a Bad War. But does that mean it was morally bad? Or was it bad merely in the sense that Japan lost? Kimitsu shows no such ambiguity. He sees the war as fundamentally morally wrong. But most of the time he does not think of the war in those terms. He is more interested in the strength/weakness axis. So when it comes to the holocaust, he thinks like this:

Jewish people = weak people = himself = object of sympathy

Nazis = strong people = other = object of awe

Maybe "awe" is putting it a bit strong. The other day I asked Kimitsu if he thought that was fair comment. He said, "I'll admit to curiosity."

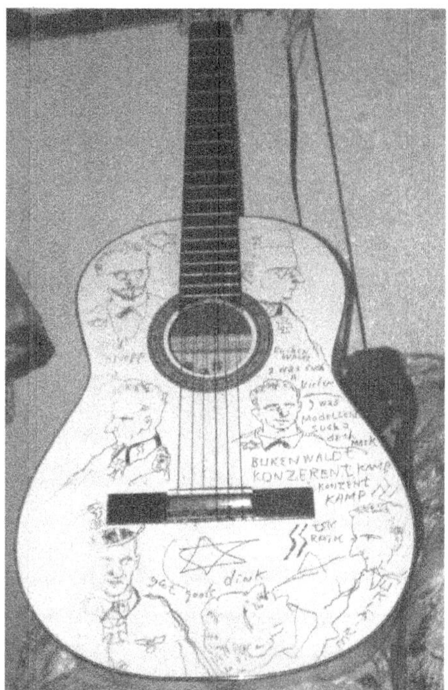

Figure 5.2. Kimitsu's guitar.

Let us take a closer look at the acoustic guitar that Kimitsu used to strum in his room (figure 5.2). Around the hole in the middle he has drawn figures of four men. On the upper right and lower left are two elite SS officers, clearly indicated as such with the SS insignia on their collars and the Iron Cross. When Kimitsu draws Nazis, they are nearly always SS officers, particularly powerful and brutal by reputation. On the top left and bottom right he has drawn Jewish men identifiable by the Star of David, which they were of course obliged to wear as a badge of shame in Nazi Germany. The physical appearance of the Jews and Nazis is very similar—after all, they are all Caucasians. I asked Kimitsu if this was an implied critique of Nazi race theories but he soberly insisted he was just not very good at drawing. Yet there are differences between Kimitsu's Jews and Nazis. The Jews are drawn in three-quarter view, the Nazis in profile. The Jews have an expression mingling defiance and apprehension, where the Nazis are stern or expressionless. The Nazis are anonymous but the Jews have names, tantalizingly not quite legible.[18] Around the bottom-right Jew is written *Buchenwaldz; I was such a victim; I was modellen [modelling] such a deth [death] mask.* He may have got the images and words from a book—he says he did, but cannot recall the title. Under the bridge of the guitar is another Nazi and two more figures, probably Jews, from Ukraine, and another SS logo with *CSK Rain* (or is it TSK?) written next to it. The composition below the bridge is dominated by a Star of David with the words *get gook dink* written under it. "Gook" and "dink" are both American military slang for East Asians generally (gook) and North Vietnamese particularly (dink). Assuming that "get" means "kill", this shifts the focus from Nazi victimization of Jews to American atrocities in East Asia, and especially Vietnam.

I cannot understand all the details, but at least we can see that Nazis and Jews are symmetrically opposed symbols in Kimitsu's system of thought; with Americans and Japanese/Koreans/Vietnamese as a subset of the same system. The American atomic bombings of Japan and atrocities in Korea and Vietnam align them with the Nazis in an echo of Kimitsu's childhood inability to tell them apart.

Further insight comes from the image on p. 89 of Adolf Eichmann's failed attempt to achieve enlightenment, being held back by the interference (*gaienryō*) caused by his bad deeds, represented by three of the Jewish prisoners for whose death he was responsible. Though depicted far smaller in stature than Eichmann, the Jewish prisoners seem able by pooling their strength to prevent the Nazis' ascent. It is fascinating to see the interplay between good/evil and strong/weak here. The reason for Eichmann's inability to ascend is moral—his wicked deeds. Yet the drawing represents that wickedness as physical weakness, morality as dynamics. The smallness of the Jewish prisoners connotes weakness, not moral inferiority. The fact that they are able to restrain Eichmann by pooling their strength shows that there is still some hope for humanity in Kimitsu's generally bleak worldview. It is not simply a matter of the strong preying on the weak.

After the war, American soldiers inherited the awe that Kimitsu felt toward the Nazis. He calls them his "ideal of manhood. They gave me bubblegum, too" (p. 43). Later, he enjoys serving in the Self Defense Force in part because he knows that if any real fighting has to be done, they can leave it to the Americans. He and his SDF comrades are really just playing at soldiers. They are like boys; the Americans are real men. Stationed at a base vacated by the US military, he is impressed by the size of the library (p. 46). He flirts with the idea that these supermen might have intellectual, as well as physical superiority. Later, this intellectual aspect of American power gives way to a stress on pure violence as he dwells upon American serial murderers.

Clearly Kimitsu has a mighty *gaijin konpurekkusu* (foreigner complex). No less powerful is his complex regarding women. He feels at home in the SDF because it is an all-male society, which he calls a "society of knights" (p. 45). He feels confused in the presence of women, and can barely even talk to them unless drunk. He admits to never having had sex without paying for it. Institutionalized prostitution is often cited by feminists as a manifestation of men's exploitation of women, but to Kimitsu it signifies male weakness—since they are the ones lonely and desperate enough to pay for sex. He repeatedly refers to Japan as a "matrilineal society"—a debatable assertion, clearly incorrect in relation to contemporary Japan, although the idea that Japan was a matrilineal society before the influence of China set in is supported by some scholars.[19] We may take this expression as a shorthand for Kimitsu's image of Japan as a society in which men can never defeat women (p. 67), so that on his axis of strength and weakness it is clear that men are weak and women strong. This leads to some interesting insights: for example, that it is men's awareness that they cannot defeat women that leads them to act violently towards women (ibid.). That rings true, and not just for Japan.

He also argues that America and Britain are patrilineal societies in which children are largely brought up by the father. That is certainly not the literal truth, but Kimitsu uses it to mean that American and British men are influenced more by their fathers, Japanese men more by their mothers. His erroneous view of childrearing in the US and UK is forced upon him by his determination to think in broad, structural terms. The wartime weakness of Japanese men vis-à-vis the enemy he associates with their weakness vis-à-vis women, especially their mothers. (I have heard it said that Japanese soldiers dying on the battlefield in World War II would call out not to the emperor but to their mothers.) Anglo-American men won the war, and therefore must have a different relationship with their mothers, explicable only by being brought up by their fathers. A further extension of Kimitsu's structuralist thinking relates national character to eating habits, with the meat-eating Americans inevitably prevailing over the fish-and-rice-eating Japanese.

On top of the heavy burden of manhood, Kimitsu has had to cope with the extra burden of being the oldest son of his family. He is intensely aware of his failure to achieve a glorious career, and ashamed of his inability to prevent the death of his one of his younger brothers in a traffic accident (p. 58). In childhood, he bullied his little brothers like an "emperor" or "A-class war criminal." So often we find this parallel between his own private life and the events of World War II. How ironic that sixty years later, he should have acquired the nickname "Hitler" among his friends in Kotobuki (p. 43).

For Kimitsu, the Japanese equivalent of Hitler is Shōkō Asahara, the charismatic leader of the Aum Shinrikyō cult which launched the sarin gas attack on the Tokyo subway on March 20, 1995. Just three days later I asked Kimitsu why he thought Asahara had done this crazy thing. From very humble origins, he had achieved a position where he had hundreds of adoring followers, tremendous wealth, and unlimited access to sexual partners. He threw that all away and got himself the death sentence. Kimitsu replied thus:

> Well, after a man has got everything he wants in the way of money and sex, the next thing he wants is authority, is power. Look at Hitler. It's no coincidence that Asahara chose a weapon—sarin gas—first invented by Hitler's scientists. And like Hitler, he chose to strike when national confidence was at a low ebb. For Hitler it was the collapse of the Weimar Republic; for Asahara it was the collapse of the LDP government, the collapse of the bubble economy, and then the Kobe earthquake. I think the attack was carefully planned. And it was targeted at Kasumigaseki, home of the bureaucracy, because he really thought, somehow, that he was going to destroy the existing authorities and take their place himself.[20]

The subsequent investigation proved that Kimitsu's assessment was quite correct.

Hitler, he confidently states, is in hell. As for new religions, he calls them "religious cults peddling their groundless beliefs to people who feel weak and tired" (p. 50). And yet, recalling the intellectual high of first encountering Colin Wilson's *Outsider*, he refers to Wilson as "my Shōkō Asahara" (p. 68). It's a metaphor, of course. Even so it is suggestive that he should think of Asahara to describe the sensation of being overwhelmed by a powerful intellect. It shows an acute awareness of his own weakness, and of his need for a powerful guru.

This awareness of weakness is also manifest in Kimitsu's interest in "affordance." When J. J. Gibson developed affordance theory, he was thinking of the verb "afford" in the sense that a window affords a view (cf p. 50 above). However good our eyes may be, we cannot see through a wall unless a window affords that possibility. Thus human free will is everywhere constrained by its environment. In the straitened circumstances of Japan after defeat in World War II, the "everyday affordance" allowed "no time-outs"—

no space to reflect on the present or dream of the future. A symbol he often evokes is that of the lion. He describes his schoolboy life as "a deer about to be eaten by a lion" (p. 44). Later he remarks "When a child gets born in the natural world, it has to be protected from lions. There are no walls in the house to afford protection. And when I was a kid, there was no affordance for me to think about the higher things; in the post-war chaos, we just had to struggle for survival every day" (p. 50). Speaking of the left-wing student movement, he remarks upon their privileged middle-class upbringing. In contrast, "we workers were confronting lions, just living from day to day on nature's affordance" (p. 62). The lion is a symbol for the risks confronting humankind in pre-civilized, or under-civilized, social environments. There were no real lions in early post-war Japan, of course, but the metaphorical lions of poverty, hunger and violence were ever-present. With affordance so constrained, day laborers literally had to "live for the day."[21] Meanwhile, men who commit outrages, such as the Virginia Tech shooter (55, 60–61, 65), are still futilely battling imaginary lions, although modern-day affordance has for the most part taken the lions away.

Kimitsu has spent a lifetime running from the lions, in pursuit of the leisure to think and dream. He can endure poverty, and the absence of marriage and family life, but at least he wants the material freedom to have a drink and read a book. The post-war Japanese economic miracle made it possible for a man with few qualifications or special skills to make a basic living out of dock work or construction without having to work every day. It was that "affordance" that enabled Kimitsu to develop his characteristic way of thinking about the world. His lifestyle gave him more time to read books and reflect than many university professors are afforded.

Kimitsu's version of affordance theory also helps to explain why he did not hesitate to apply for welfare when the opportunity arose. Some people—probably not that many—are too proud to go on welfare and be "a burden on the state." That was never Kimitsu's problem. To him, welfare was just another source of sustenance, part of the affordance of the modern state, and he had no hesitation in applying. Since he believes at the most ontological level that people are not free or independent, the question of whether they depend upon a company for a pay check or on the government for a welfare payment is of no significance.

But although Kimitsu views nearly all people as being limited to living within the afforded limits, just occasionally, someone comes along who violates that rule—a superman. A superman, instead of being made by his environment, makes his environment. Adolf Hitler and Shōkō Asahara refused to accept what had been afforded them. They wanted more, they took more. In a world of passive objects, they tried to become active subjects. Hence Kimitsu's enduring fascination with these men. Hence, too, his fascination with serial killers like Charles Whitman and Richard Speck. In terms of good and evil, they were among the worst. In terms of weakness and strength, they were obscure individuals who suddenly and drastically changed the environment around them. For an instant they changed from weakness to strength and violated the boundaries of affordance. In that moment, for Kimitsu, they became like twisted supermen.[22]

What about Kimitsu's own criminal activities? Minor offences like fare-dodging on the trains he justifies as being crimes against the authority of the impersonal state (which as an anti-authoritarian he despises), not against a fellow human being. As he puts it (p. 32), "There's no fun in paying out big fares, right? Because your adversary is the representative of authority—and you have to resist authority." These anti-authority acts may also be read as modest attempts to push the envelope of the affordance around him.

It is harder to explain the knife assault that brought him two-and-a-half years in prison. This was supposed to be retribution for the theft of Kimitsu's money and driving license a month earlier, but Kimitsu admits himself that he is not sure whether the man he assaulted really was the thief. Yet again relating his personal life to the war, he calls his action "strategic bombing." In the personal war that is Kimitsu's life, the man was already classified as an enemy because Kimitsu knew him to be a bad man who hung out with a den of thieves (p. 71). In war, sometimes the wrong person gets hurt—unavoidable collateral damage.

Since that sounds so crazy, I recently asked Kimitsu about the incident again. "It's the thing I most regret in my entire life," he said. "When I realized what terrible wounds I'd inflicted, I was shocked. It was unforgiveable." Though contrite about resorting to violence, at no point did Kimitsu mention qualms over the possibility that he might have stabbed the wrong man. I am reminded of the life of Kenzō Okuzaki (1920–2005), the star of Kazuo Hara's controversial 1987 documentary *Yuki-yukite Shingun* (The Emperor's Naked Army Marches On). While fighting in the Imperial Army in World War II, Okuzaki became convinced that the senior officers of his unit in Papua New Guinea had had two of his comrades executed and then cannibalized them. His enquiries during the film convince him that this was the case, and at the end of the film he goes to the house of one of the officers with a gun, planning to kill him. But the old man is out, and the door is answered by his son. Frustrated, Okuzaki shoots the son instead (luckily he survived, while Okuzaki was imprisoned for attempted murder). The point in common with Kimitsu's assault case is that revenge is taken not against an individual, but against a class—for Okuzaki, the class of commanding officers, including their families; for Kimitsu, members of the den of thieves in Kotobuki.

Kimitsu reveals a somewhat similar pattern of thought on p.73, when he says of the prostitutes in Susukino who inflicted pain on his manhood that "I couldn't help feeling that what they were doing was somehow revenge for

Jack the Ripper." Again, the distinction between revenge on an individual and revenge on a class is blurred.

This reminds one of another word Kimitsu often uses: ressentiment. This term, used by Nietzsche to denote the hatred felt by the weak toward the strong, is another case of anger directed at a class rather than an individual. On p. 80 Kimitsu says that it was his fate to become a humble day laborer, so he has no ressentiment. That may well be so now—Kimitsu has mellowed. But maybe there was some ressentiment driving his knife on that leaden day in June, the "strong" in this case being not the rulers of society, but a fellow day laborer in a position of relative strength because of his physical size and his association with bully boys who could intimidate and exploit other workers. Or to use a Kimitsu-style metaphor, this was ressentiment not against a general but against a sergeant, whom he views as class traitors because they bully fellow working-class men (p. 46).

One of the long-running slogans in the day laborer movement is *yarareta-ra yarikaese*, "if they get you, get "em back." The slogan consists of two verbs and no nouns to make it explicit who is to be got back at by whom. Presumably the Marxist activists who took up the slogan were thinking of the working class getting revenge against the bourgeoisie—but neither Okuzaki nor Kimitsu have quite that kind of orthodox Marxist consciousness. Their struggle is not of individual against individual, nor of class against class, but of individual against class. That is what makes their actions appear crazy to most people. I do not defend either action, but merely wish to suggest that they are the product of a kind of logical system.

Re-reading my own words above, I fear I have given the impression that Kimitsu Nishikawa is a very queer fellow indeed. That is not fair to him. I find him a friendly, outgoing man with an appealing, self-deprecating wit. He loves to joke about his own weakness, and takes an innocent intellectual delight in the free association of words and ideas. Even when speaking of his own death, he jokingly looks forward to having his remains tossed out on the slopes of Mount Fuji to become a "buzzard's dessert" (p. 75). In Japanese, that expression nearly rhymes: *bazādo no dezāto*. He sees life as neither tragedy nor comedy, but as "omoshiro-okashii"—literally, "interesting and funny" (see chapter 3 note 37). Both halves of that word hover in meaning between "amusing" and "peculiar."

What makes life interesting for him? He may have no family, no wife, no job, and no money, but at least he has books and the sea. He has an intellectual curiosity, which he satisfies in libraries and second-hand bookshops. When everyday life is tough, he escapes to the world of ideas. He loves abstract, theoretical ideas, always looking for links between concepts from philosophy, sociology, mathematics, and natural science.

As for the sea, it has various meanings for him. First it means the joy of working on the docks. Stevedoring can be backbreaking labor, but the chance to meet all sorts of foreign ship hands, and the sense of solidarity among fellow dock workers, more than makes up for that. Note the exuberance in his account of unloading a Brazilian freighter: "I felt as if I were connected to Brazil, and I really felt like diving into the sea and swimming to Brazil" (p. 52).

At a deeper level, "We humans are water-based animals. So the sea has a calming effect on us. Rivers won't do. You still feel a little insecure with a river" (p. 55). The sea, then, is a sacred place. Hence when Kimitsu is listing his heroes, alongside Dostoevsky and Maugham we find the names of yachtsman adventurers like Francis Chichester and Robin Knox-Johnston (p. 38). At first glance it seems a random mélange, but for Kimitsu the sea is a metaphor for boundless knowledge, and the adventurer in his little boat is on a conceptual level alongside the thinker who voyages in quest of knowledge.

Kimitsu himself has never left Japan. His conversation roams across Tibet, Arizona, Brazil, and the East End of London, but these are all imagined constructs. He is a longshoreman who observes the sea from the wharf. Perhaps there is a parallel there with the fact that he is a voracious reader but never a writer. He is an observer. Neither an abject victim nor an aggressive agent, he has found a space in between that feels like his right place.

Tom Gill
Oiso, October 24, 2014

Figure 5.3. Kimitsu Nishikawa, Christmas 2005.

NOTES

1. The name on the cover of the book is Oyama Shiro, using the Japanese style of giving surname before personal name. But I have adopted Western order in the present volume.

2. Nowadays the declining birth rate means that a majority of Japanese boys are eldest sons. But the men in my sample were from a generation when the average family had five or six children, so that 40 percent was well above what could be expected from a random distribution. Since the eldest son is supposed to stay at home and inherit the family household, it was a surprise to find so many of them in the doya-gai.

3. Gill, *Men of Uncertainty*, pp. 191–198.

4. Gill, *Men of Uncertainty*, p. 192.

5. See their home page at http://www.haken-union.jp/index.html.

6. http://www.haken-union.jp/first.html.

7. See report by Haken Rōdō Nettowāku (Dispatch Labor Network), p.13 http://haken-net.or.jp/modules/news/article.php?storyid=74#.VC99EhZTCSo.

8. Ibid. p. 13. Both groups earn about 1,200 yen an hour at age 20, but regular workers earn about 3,000 yen in their 40s and 50s while dispatch workers are still making just 1,200 yen.

9. Kokuritsu Shakai Hoshō Jinkō Mondai Kenkyūjo (National Institute of Population and Social Security Research), *Shakai Hoshō Tōkei Nenpō* (Annual Report on Social Security Statistics), 2014 edition. Available on-line at http://www.ipss.go.jp/s-toukei/j/t_nenpo_back/libr_new.html. The number of people enrolled in day labourer unemployment insurance is simply stated as "20,000," with no explanation for the very round number, out of 38,913,000 people enrolled in some form of unemployment insurance.

10. There used to be a system of health insurance for day laborers too (*hiyatoi kenkō hoken*), but it was scrapped in 1984. The premium was much higher and the system was widely ignored by employers.

11. Source as for note 9. Kokuritsu Shakai Hoshō Jinkō Mondai Kenkyūjo (National Institute of Population and Social Security Research), *Shakai Hoshō Tōkei Nenpō* (Annual Report on Social Security Statistics), 2014 edition, p. 75.

12. Sato, Hiroki, "Atypical Employment: A Source of Flexible Work Opportunities?" *Social Science Japan Journal* (2001) 4 (2): 161–181. Labor economists like Sato prefer to speak of "atypical" rather than "irregular" employment.

13. The annual count is conducted by the Ministry of Health, Labor and Welfare, and is displayed at the MHLW's home page: http://www.mhlw.go.jp. The 2014 data is available at http://www.mhlw.go.jp/stf/houdou/0000044589.html.

14. National Alliance to End Homelessness, *The State of Homelessness in America 2014*. http://www.endhomelessness.org/library/entry/the-state-of-homelessness-2014. This survey is conducted annually by an alliance of over 400 organizations dedicated to fighting homelessness.

15. See Michael Stoops, "The Controversial 'Safety Net'" (1981–2012). http://nationalhomeless.org/WordPress/2012/04/the-controversial-safety-net/.

16. Calculated by the author, using reports from the Kanagawa prefecture home page, at http://www.pref.kanagawa.jp/cnt/f430057/.

17. The Gini data is calculated at three year intervals by the Ministry of Health, Labor and Welfare. It is handily summarized in this *Nihon Keizai Shinbun* article: "Shotoku kakusa no zesei susumu: saihaibun, shakai hoshō de kaizen" (Correction of income differentials progresses: redistribution improved by social security). *Nihon Keizai Shinbun*, October 11, 2013. http://www.nikkei.com/article/DGXNASFS1103J_R11C13A0EE8000/.

18. David ~off? Kucher Waitz? I have tried in vain to trace these names.

19. See for example Itsue Takamure's 1938 study of ancient matrilineality, *Bokeisei no kenkyū: Dainihon joseishi 1*, (The Study of Matrilineal systems: A History of Women in Great Japan, Vol. 1). This work is controversial but has its supporters.

20. Field note, Thursday March 23, 1995.

21. Working for the day, living for the day—these are lifestyles attuned to the well-documented awareness in Japanese culture of *mono no aware* (the fleetingness of things) and

setsunashugi (living for the moment), powerful tropes that remind us that day laborers, no less than salarymen, are inheritors of Japanese tradition.

22. I should add that Kimitsu was also influenced on this point by one of his heroes, Colin Wilson, who wrote several books about serial killers.

Index

About the Author

Tom Gill is professor of social anthropology at the Faculty of International Studies of Meiji Gakuin University, Yokohama campus. His research interests include marginal labor, homelessness, and masculinity. He has written many papers in English and Japanese on these topics and one book—*Men of Uncertainty: the Social Organization of Day Laborers in Contemporary Japan* (State University of New York Press, 2001). He has hung out with homeless men in Japan, the US, and the UK. Since 2011, he has also been doing fieldwork whenever possible with victims of the Fukushima nuclear disaster. He is the co-editor, with Brigitte Steger and David H. Slater, of *Japan Copes with Calamity: Ethnographies of the Earthquake, Tsunami and Nuclear Disasters of March 2011* (Peter Lang, 2013).